THE BROKEN IMAGE

What a relief to find a writer who brings psychological needs under the power of the Cross of Christ. This is a book full of hope for the homosexual, but with far wider implications for all of us. A book about *redemption!*

Elisabeth Elliot

Leanne Payne is a wise woman. She has read what needs to be read on the topic she addresses; she has thought deeply about it all; she has tested what she has read in the light of her own courageous and profound experience of life—and of helping countless people with their lives; and above all, she speaks under the authority of God, whose Word she clearly takes absolutely seriously, and whom she knows as very few people seem to know Him.

Thomas Howard

Few things are more needed in our world today than healing: healing of broken hearts, broken homes, broken lives. Leanne Payne presents an honest, penetrating, authentic, and above all, compassionate approach to restoring wholeness through believing prayer. Her approach is firmly grounded in the Scriptures. While the immediate subject matter relates to the problem of homosexuality, its application goes far beyond that to give new hope to all who need healing in today's wounded world. I heartily recommend this book.

David M. Howard

There are at least three groups of people who will profit by reading *The Broken Image*—those with a homosexual orientation, those who minister to them, and those who can respond to homosexual behavior only with fear and condemnation. Leanne Payne explores—with case studies and theological reflection—the power of God to heal those crippled by severe emotional and spiritual trauma.

This is a compassionate book, and at the same time, a hopeful one—compassionate because the author's love for those to whom she ministers shines through with great clarity—hopeful, because she offers strong evidence that those in whom the image of God has been broken (i.e., all of us!) may expect grace not simply to cope with unfortunate circumstances, but to have The Broken Image made whole again.

Bishop William C. Frey

The Broken Image

Restoring Sexual Wholeness Through Healing Prayer

Leanne Payne

KINGSWAY PUBLICATIONS
EASTBOURNE

First published in USA by
Crossway Books, Westchester, Illinois 60153

First British edition 1988
Reprinted 1989, 1992, 1994, 1997

ISBN 0-86065-641-1

Produced by Bookprint Creative Services,
P.O. Box 827, BN21 3YJ, England for
KINGSWAY PUBLICATIONS LTD
Lottbridge Drove, Eastbourne, E. Sussex BN23 6NT.
Printed in Great Britain
Reproduced from the original typesetting by
arrangement with Crossway Books.

This book is dedicated:

To all who have endured or even now suffer the homosexual identity crisis, especially those who have feared there was no help to be found.

And also to Carol Kraft, an especially fine professor of the German language and literature, and an even finer prayer partner and minister of God's healing love. Without her prayerful encouragement, undergirded with all the practical support that a true love and commitment to Christ brings, the ministry I exercise would be far more difficult—and the poorer.

CONTENTS

Acknowledgements 9

Foreword by Martin Hallett 11

Preface 13

1. Lisa's Story: Repressed Memory 15

2. The Causes of Homosexuality: Contemporary
   Theories.. 33

3. Matthew's Story: Identity Crisis 39

4. The Search for Sexual Identity 65

5. The Identity Crisis According
   to the Scriptures....................................... 137

6. Listening for the Healing Word 143

Appendix: Listening to Our Dreams.................... 167

Notes... 181

Acknowledgments

My gratitude to Agnes Sanford simply for having been and for continuing to be (still at age 83!) who she is. She has been a magnificent trailblazer in the art of healing prayer. I wish to thank her also for her generous permission when last we met to quote her in the pages of this book.

My thanks go also to the Rt. Rev. Bennett J. Sims, Herman Riffel, Barbara Shlemon, Philip Vaswig, and Fr. Alan Jones for their kind permission to quote them, and to Walter Hooper for his generous permission to publish the letters of C. S. Lewis to Sheldon Vanauken and Mr. Masson.

Finally, I am grateful to all who prayerfully encouraged me in the writing of this book. Though scattered in a line from the northernmost coastal waters of British Columbia to the warm southeastern coast of Florida, they are all one in their Lord and in prayer to Him. Bob and Ann Siegel, Rhoda Hegberg, Ted and Lucy Smith, and Bernie Klamecki are adventurers in prayer I've especially leaned on. To God be all our thanks and praise.

Copyright Acknowledgements

Appreciation is expressed for permission to quote from the following:

John Gaynor Banks, *The Master and the Disciples* (© by Macalester Park Publishing Company).

Ruth Tiffany Barnhouse, *Homosexuality: A Symbolic Confusion*
(© 1977 by The Seabury Press, Inc.).

Oswald Chambers, *My Utmost for His Highest* (© by Dodd, Mead and Company).

Emma Curtis Hopkins, *High Mysticism* (© by DeVorss).

Frank Lake, *Clinical Theology* (© 1966 by Darton, Longman and Todd).

C. S. Lewis, *Mere Christianity* (© 1943, 1945, 1952 by Macmillan).

C. S. Lewis, *Reflections on the Psalms* (© by William Collins).

C. S. Lewis, *The Weight of Glory* (© by Eerdmans).

Henri Nouwen, *Reaching Out* (© 1975 by Henri Nouwen; used by permission of Doubleday & Company).

Michael Scanlan, *Inner Healing* (© by Paulist Press).

Aleksandr Solzhenitsyn, *The Gulag Archipelago* (© 1974 by author; English translation © 1975 by Harper and Row; used by permission of Harper and Row).

Walter Trobisch, *Love Yourself* (© by Inter-Varsity Press).

Foreword

The subject of sexuality usually provokes more heat than light, especially when discussed among Christians. Yet, as Leanne Payne makes clear, the sexual problem is only the sympton of unmet needs, unresolved hurts, a search for personal identity. Healing from homosexual and hetero-sexual problems can be experienced as the Holy Spirit leads us towards wholeness and completeness in Christ. This will be experienced in many different ways. As some-one from a homosexual background myself and now ministering in this area, I can identify with the true stories in this book. Those of us in this area of ministry around the world owe a great deal to Leanne's ministry, both personally and through her books. Her scholarly approach and deep spiritual insights to our personalities should gain her much respect from many quarters. Some of her tech-niques may draw criticism, but the results of lives trans-formed by God and for God cannot be denied.

Each person's experience of life, with its joys, hurts and pain is unique, and therefore God's path of healing for all of us will be equally unique. I pray that this challenging and exciting book of God's love and healing power will help you to understand more about yourself and others. May it give you the hope and determination to walk down God's path of healing for yourself, whatever your sexuality may be. For as Leanne says, "Truly to write of the healing of the homosexual is to write of the healing of all persons everywhere."

Change is always possible with God—to Him be the Glory!

Martin Hallett
Director, True Freedom Trust

Preface

As a sexual neurosis, homosexuality is regarded as one of the most complex. As a condition for God to heal, it is (in spite of the widespread belief to the contrary) remarkably simple. This is a book about how to pray for the healing of the problem.

The stories in this book were selected as being the most representative among those to whom I minister. Details such as names and places are changed in order to protect the persons whose inner lives are here opened to view. Within these personal histories we see classic examples of injuries that can lead to the homosexual crisis in identity.

None of these stories was lightly or easily written, for I stand in awe of what it means to be a human being, one in the process of becoming:

> It is a serious thing to live in a society of possible gods and goddesses, to remember that the dullest and most uninteresting person you talk to may one day be a creature which, if you saw it now, you would be strongly tempted to worship, or else a horror and a corruption such as you now meet, if at all, only in a nightmare. All day long we are, in some degree, helping each other to one or other of these destinations. It is in the light of these overwhelming possibilities, it is with the

awe and the circumspection proper to them, that we should conduct all our dealings with one another, all friendships, all loves, all play, all politics. There are no *ordinary* people. You have never talked to a mere mortal.[1]

I am also in awe of what it means to be a Christian disciple. A follower of Him is one who has himself been unchained and is then, by virtue of His Presence within, commissioned to take the chains off others. In so doing, there is the responsibility for guarding inviolate the essential mystery and integrity of the souls to whom one ministers. The stories on the following pages are of persons exceedingly dear to me. In their *becoming*, each has in his or her own unique way turned to bless and strengthen me.

One

Lisa's Story: Repressed Memory

Lisa, a tall and lovely blonde girl, came to church services where I was speaking on Christ's power to banish the fears and heal the sorrows of the deep heart—those that cripple and paralyze our emotional and feeling being. I also shared how Christ can bring peace and light where before there was only pain and darkness. As she sat through the several lectures, she began to hope once again that something could be done for herself. All her life she had known mental and emotional pain, and had in at least two suicide attempts plunged dangerously deep into the dark waters of hopelessness and despair. At the end of the messages I asked the Lord to be with us in all His healing power, and to bring up from the corners of the deep mind such memories as not only needed healing, but could be properly dealt with in a group of several hundred people. As this began to happen, and Jesus began to heal those present, nothing at all seemed to happen in Lisa.

The next day a hopeless and apathetic voice spoke to me through the wires of the parsonage phone. "I came to your meeting," she said, "and nothing happened." I sensed her deep need and knew that she was one whose memories and heart the Lord would need to guard in a public service. I always ask Him to. He knows exactly what can come up and be ministered to in a group, and I am careful to ask Him to let nothing too painful and too deep come up where there might not be the privacy needed, or the one gifted and experienced in helping such a sufferer close at hand. Her next words confirmed my feeling that she was indeed one of these.

"I had a dream last night, after the service, one I have often had," she said. "I looked down and saw my arm, and the pores of the skin over it were like a fish net. Under this skin I saw what I always see in this dream—a black cancerous mass." This dream graphically revealed how Lisa perceived her inner self. No wonder the dark memories behind such a perception of her inner being had not come up in the group. She attempted to take her life recently. As a medical student, having the know-how as well as access to the drugs, she had very nearly succeeded. In an intensive care unit for seven days, swelled and bloated to twice her size, she was unrecognizable to her own family, who were told she could not live. She did live, however; but when she regained consciousness, she was told that the overdose had permanently damaged her mind. The circumstances of her recent past thus bore out the seriousness of her dream, and what it was saying.

Some dreams indicate particularly dangerous "material" in the deep mind, and when these are told on the psychoanalyst's couch, he knows to proceed with caution. So also does the minister who would pray for the healing of memories for such a one. Although no prayer for healing of the soul is ever to be undertaken either presumptuously or lightly, I knew that prayer for the healing of Lisa would require extraordinary caution in listening to and collaborating with the Holy Spirit. At the same time, I anticipated with joy what I knew God would do. This faith no one may ever boast of, for it is truly a gift given for the moment. When God sends us on a mission, He empowers us with the faith and the confidence to do what He has sent us to do. So I invited Lisa to the parsonage where I was staying. I assured her that our Lord would enter into and light up with His healing Presence the darkness in her deep mind out of which recurred such a dream.

When she arrived I quickly discovered more of her story, including the history of a lesbian relationship in childhood. She had never been happy as a child, and had been desperately lonely. Though reared in the home with both parents, she was severely estranged from them. Her mother, reacting to this emotional barrier on Lisa's part, had become increasingly jealous and dominating where her daughter was concerned. Also, the mother's behavior grew increasingly neurotic, a situation that often caused embarrassment to Lisa. Her father was simply remote and unknowable, one who would bring her a toy now and then. She early realized her father's behavior in respect to herself to be one that her mother would not allow to be otherwise. Even so, she felt no desire to be close to either, and stolidly resisted her mother's attempts to gain her affection and loyalty. She was therefore even more vulnerable than the ordinary child, and in the summer following her graduation from the sixth grade she fell into the hands of a lesbian schoolteacher.

Her junior high school years were dominated and haunted by this relationship. Unable to extricate herself from what she knew to be wrong, she began to break mentally and emotionally. At this point, she told a school counselor of her relationship to the teacher and was immediately sent to a psychiatrist. Before she reached the tenth grade she had seen two psychiatrists and though free of the former relationship, had begun taking tranquilizers and smoking cigarettes. By that time, the thing had become known, and Lisa, always a lonely girl, was throughout her high school years lonelier than ever. From her classmates she experienced sharp rejection, and the vicious remarks that go along with an adolescent situation such as this. Even harder to take, though, were the frantic efforts of an estranged and emotionally ill mother to somehow right the terrible events in her daughter's life. She forbade her to have friendships with girls (by then a slight possibility for her anyway), and constantly pushed the issue of dating boys, a prospect that terrified Lisa. It is small wonder that by the summer after graduation from high school her dependence on drugs had escalated, and Lisa was seeking more and more avenues of escape.

Lisa's interest in studies had always provided her with a genuinely constructive and creative escape from the pressures of her terrible loneliness, and even in the worst of times she did well in them. The college she chose therefore readily accepted her into their premed program. By this time she was suffering from black depression and unable to face life without drugs. Even so, she completed her liberal arts studies and proceeded on to medical school. The inevitable end to such an existence was close at hand, however, and six weeks after entering, depressed and unable to sleep, she took the overdose that very nearly ended her life.

As Lisa slowly recovered from the suicide attempt, she knew deep within herself that there was no help for her outside of God. As a six-year-old, she had attended Sunday school and had asked Jesus to come into her heart. She had always wanted to know Him. In the summer before going to college she had, as a heavy drug abuser, found a Christian coffeehouse; but, unable to endure the inner psychic pain without drugs, she did not retain the help and encouragement she got there. Now she was faced with the fact that she was still alive and that, in addition to the same old darkness within, her mind was not the same. As she once again reached out to God, into her troubled mind came the idea of contacting a Christian center ministering to young people involved with drugs and the occult.

As a loving Providence would have it, when she phoned this center she reached a little woman brimful of faith who assured her that there was help for her mind as well as for spirit and body. This Lisa desperately needed to hear. Encouraged by the joyful expectancy in this little lady, Lisa asked to be admitted to the program there.

By the time I met her, she had been in this center for five or six months and had come to love dearly the little faith-filled housemother. She clung to her as tenaciously as a drowning man to a lifeline. I could see this without being told, for she had brought her newfound "Mom" with her to the parsonage, one whose work-weary frame and posture testified of the sleepless nights so often her lot in the work she was called to do. Her blonde, curly head nodded vigorously and thoughtfully, however, in affirmation of Lisa as she told her story. Her face glowed (I knew she was praying) with confidence that God was going to do something wonderful for Lisa, though she was not at all sure what "healing of memories" was about.

The Prayer for Healing of Memories

With her story as a starter, we then settled ourselves comfortably on the rug with our backs to a cushioned sofa. I anointed her with oil, and laying hands on her forehead I asked our Lord whose Presence I had already invoked to go back in time through her memories to the moment of conception. I prayed for her even then, as she *was* in that moment, and then for her as she grew through the months in her mother's womb. I prayed for her in the hour of her birth, to see if the memory might be found that would explain her estrangement from parents and the darkness she knew within. But nothing amiss was revealed there. Shortly after this, however, I made the discovery that her first five years of life were blanked out from memory. Painfully conscious of later memories with all their attendant misery and guilt, those all too easy to recall, Lisa seemed unconcerned that she could not recall the earlier years. But with the *knowing* that is a gift from God, I knew that the key or root memory was locked up in the repressed memory bank of her first five years.

There are many who remember little of their early years and

have no repressed traumatic memories—perhaps their lives were simply slow and uneventful; there were no extraordinary joys on the one hand, nor great anxieties on the other. In contrast to these, there are those whose early years, lived out in unloving and deadly dull circumstances, are captured in their memories as what I can best describe as long, gray blurs. The memory is tonal in nature, an aura of sadness is there, but no memory of particularly traumatic events haunts either the conscious or the deep mind. A case such as this needs special prayers for healing too. But this was not Lisa's case, and I, by the Spirit of God, knew this.[1]

I therefore asked the Lord to bring up the memory from these five years that lay behind the fear and darkness she knew in her soul—that is, in her emotional and feeling being. The root memory does not always come up first, but often the memory that *leads* to it, and this was so in Lisa's case. In the first scene she saw her mother crying. I then asked her why she was crying, and this immediately brought the root memory to the fore, a scene that told me in no uncertain language why Lisa felt alienated from her parents and unable to receive their love.

As this memory began to come up to a level of conscious awareness she cried out, "Oh no! Oh no! I can't stand it." This memory had been repressed because she could not live with it. As I reminded her softly but firmly that Jesus was present to enter into it and heal it, she was able to let the traumatic memory come fully into consciousness.

The Root Memory

She was three years or perhaps a little older in this memory, and her own father was sexually abusing her by forcing her into acts of fellatio.[2] Her mother walked into the room and in her hysteria, rather than handling the situation with the father and comforting the child, grabbed the little girl and threw her across the room against the wall. Her father's words to her mother then boomed out and resounded once again through her head: "Aw! She'll never remember!" And this is exactly what happened for the next nineteen years. She forgot it until the age of twenty-two, when after a lifetime of loneliness and suffering it surfaced.

This event, though quickly suppressed, was the genesis of Lisa's estrangement from both parents. As a result of this, she was to become not only increasingly *separated* from them, but guilt-ridden. Her mother's revulsion to what had happened is certainly understandable, but it had unfortunately included her little girl. In momentary outrage and stupefaction, she had pushed the little Lisa aside in utter abhorrence as though she was not only responsible for the deed but irremediably stained by it. Though the memory was soon lost to conscious awareness, the thing lay as a cancer in Lisa's deep heart, sending up the all-pervading impression that she was guilty and somehow filthy. Her dream of looking down through the pores of her skin and seeing a black cancerous mass was a recurrent witness to the presence of this buried and unhealed memory.

This is, of course, the type of memory that the depth-psychologist goes after. Once brought to the surface, the insight it gives into the problems of that life is enormous. That alone is not enough, but *can* start the process of healing. In Lisa's case, Jesus Himself had brought up the thing that needed healing, and He Himself walked into that memory, enabling her to forgive her father, her mother, and the early circumstances of her life, releasing her from her own "grievous reactions"[3] to her parents' sin against her, and from the false guilt surrounding the entire event. His love and healing power brought peace and light where once there was a five-year span of submerged pain and darkness.

Lisa, as one may see from a letter written two and a half years after the healing, was like a new person from this day on. This is healing of memories:[4] forgiveness of sin *applied* at the level for which it was intended, that of the deep heart (mind or unconscious). She had other steps to take: those of learning how to "practice the Presence" of Jesus—the discipline of always calling to mind the truth that He was with her whether or not she could see or sense Him in any way. Thus, depending wholly upon Him, she would learn to hear the words from God that the Spirit sends, and these would replace the old negative words of self-hatred and destruction. She would come to posit her identity in Him (as all Christians need to do), and knowing herself to be God's child, would begin to love and accept herself and others aright—a most important step after the initial healing. She would learn how to relate to young men and women her own age rather than to persistently cling to motherly, older women. In short, she would have to take charge over and change a lifetime's attitudinal patterns toward herself and others—those that had been shaped and refined in the crucible of mental and emotional pain and darkness—as she learned to abide in Him. But this is a learning process, and as such, takes a little time.

Here is the account of that day in the parsonage in her own words and from her perspective:

I was afraid. I did not think it would work and thought I had really gotten into something crazy. But I knew I still needed help for future survival and I had not gotten what I needed, even after being at _____ for six months. At night, I would cry because I knew I was losing my mind. I was also in a constant cloud of depression. I could not pull my life together, no matter how much I prayed or read the Bible. I had given up (supposedly) smoking for the six months at _____, because this is one of their rules. But when I got alone, I *had* to have a cigarette. Even when I didn't have the chance to smoke, I constantly desired to have a cigarette. I got great satisfaction from smoking.

Also, I had great drives and constant thoughts of destroying myself. Mainly this thought usually turned into a drive to overdose. At times the drive was so bad, just to satisfy that compulsion, I took things that I knew would make me sick, yet not kill me. After taking the pills, the obsession with the thought would leave and after I got over making myself sick, things would be OK for awhile. I would take things like aspirins, vitamins, cold capsules, anything in tablet form. (And once, Comet—just once—that was even too yucky for an el sicko.)

So, day after day of living like this, I was ready for another chance at prayer.

As we began, you told me to picture myself in the womb. (I thought you were crazy to ask me to try to picture such a thing.) But because you sounded so serious and authoritative, I said, "OK, here I am in the womb." And at just the moment I said that, I had the best sensation I have ever had in my whole life. The sense of me being in the womb was so real. I loved it. And I knew it was just like it must have really been. And the best part, I wasn't just in the womb; I was humming in the womb. And I knew this must have been just the way I was while mother was carrying me.

You said, "Good! This shows you were loved and wanted and most likely your mother was looking forward to you being born." That made me *so* happy to hear that, because I had never realized just how much I was loved, even before I got here. It made me feel a sense of love toward my mother for wanting me so much.

Then you said, "Let's go on. Now see yourself being born." Now, on this part, I don't think I ever told you what I experienced at that point. As I was being birthed, I felt a *strong* sense of fear. I knew it was coming from my mother, and I knew it had nothing to do with the birth process, but a fear of what would happen to me now that I was in the world.

I didn't catch the full meaning of what that meant until after I had prayed and thought about it a while. I really feel like that fear was stemming from the fact my mother *knew* my father had problems, and she feared my safety because of those problems. (And I think this holds true for the most part of my life.)

So, after the birth scene, you quickly moved into Age 1 . . . 2 . . . 3 . . . 4 . . . Blank—all blank. All I saw was still, nothingness . . . no thoughts . . . blackness. This frustrated me very much, because I was beginning to enjoy seeing the memory pictures, and now . . . nothing.

I was relieved a little when I felt like you had control of the situation. You kept saying, "That's OK if you don't see anything, you will." I felt your determinedness not to quit, but to go on. I sensed you and Sr. _____ praying and "bombarding Heaven." I knew that great power was being summoned from God to "roll back the curtain of my memory." I felt like running out the door, because I felt as if I was about to lose my mind. But the power of your prayers, I knew, was working. So I didn't run. Then you called to me and said, "Lisa, what do you see? Anything? Tell me, even though it might not make any sense to you."

I saw, as if it were on a dimly lit stage, my mother sitting on the side of the bed. Her hair was tousled and messy, and she was crying in sobs and holding her face in her hands. She kept saying, "No! No! No! Why me?"

I told you I saw my mother and she was crying, but I didn't understand why (and I had dreamed this same picture over and over again my whole life). You said, "Good. Now, Lord, reveal the reason this mother is crying. Show Lisa the rest of this situation." As you said that, it was like a movie rewound in my head, and suddenly bits and pieces like puzzle pieces flew together before me and I saw my father molesting me. I couldn't believe it. I was shocked. I wanted to deny it. I felt myself saying, No! No! Please, God, no! Then I knew it was true and I knew it was real, and I felt great hatred for my father doing this to me. At that point you said, "Lisa, forgive your father." And I felt myself saying inwardly, "Yes, I must forgive him."

Then I saw my mother come into the room and begin to scream, and she grabbed me and threw me. I remember hitting against the wall and sitting against the wall. I didn't understand what was going on. I didn't understand why my mother was screaming and crying.

Then I saw my father smiling at her in a smirk-type of a smile and telling her to calm down, that she was scaring me. He kept saying, "Oh, she'll never remember! She's too little, she'll never remember."

Then my mother sat down on the bed and was crying. I

couldn't understand why she was crying. All I knew was it made me sad to see her cry. I walked over to where she was. (I was just tall enough to reach her waist while she was sitting.) I reached out to comfort her (as if to say, "What's wrong?") and as I did, she pushed me back, away from her, and said, "Stay away from me. I don't want anything to do with you." At that point I remember feeling very blank. (A feeling of nothingness—misunderstanding—being unwanted.)

It was at this point you asked me if there was anyone else that ever loved me, and I told you about my aunt. And you told me to imagine my aunt picking me up off the floor, or me crawling into her lap and allowing her to hold me. Which I did. This memory, combined with your hug, brought about the most loved, warm feeling that I have ever felt. I knew for the first time that I was loved and, most of all, that God really did love me. It was the neatest feeling ever. I felt like my insides were singing "The Hallelujah Chorus." I felt like I was dancing inside. Happiness just doesn't fit the description of what I felt. FREE! Praise the Lord!

So we ended the prayer, and my life changed completely. It really doesn't bother me to put it all down now, because it's so distant (the pain) from the happiness and joy I experienced in healing.

As I went home that night, I was walking two feet off the ground. As I lay down to go to sleep, I saw another memory. This event occurred after the first and had also been repressed.

I had a baby duck my parents had bought me, and it loved to follow me if I would walk in front of it. So, I was in the backyard riding my tricycle and the duck was chasing me. It was so much fun, and I was laughing and enjoying it. On the tricycle's handlebars my daddy had tied a pinwheel. (He always bought me pinwheels to play with.) I liked to make the wind go through them and see them turn.

So I rode the trike as fast as I could to make the pinwheel turn. And the baby duck kept up with me all the time, and kept chirping after me. So, I all of a sudden felt like I was the duck's mother. So, I wanted the duck to die. So I turned the trike at the duck and ran over it. And I killed it. My mother had been looking out the window and when she saw what I had done, she came outside and jerked the pinwheel off the trike and spanked me with it. (The duck was me, and I killed it the way I felt my mother had done to me.)

When this memory came up, I wasn't too sure it was real. I couldn't imagine myself killing an animal. So, since mother was unemotionally involved in this memory, I decided I would ask her if this really happened. I went home that weekend. And I asked her if she remembered me having a pet duck and killing it. She did. And she was quite upset that I would remember such a thing. So that was proof to me that both memories were real.

The next morning after the healing, it was like I saw the sun coming through the window for the first time in my life. I felt so in love with life. Everything was *so* colorful and beautiful. This is the first time I ever remember being happy that I was alive and had a new day.

As the day wore on, I noticed that I had *no* desire for cigarettes. Also, I didn't crave food the way I had previously. Also, no more obsession with pills. I feel like pills and smoking were a destructive part of the memory that needed healing. My mouth was misused in the molesting, and I in future years began to put objects in my mouth in destructive ways.

I feel like this event led to all of the events in my life. And that once it was healed, the *abnormal,* bad events ceased happening.

I noticed that the *severe* feelings of rejection from others that I used to feel ceased. But because this type of thinking about people had become a habit pattern of thinking, I had to retrain my thinking process. Many times my "old rejection pattern" was triggered, and I had to stop and realize that I have no reason to feel that way. I have to realize what feelings stem from the old and see that I now have new feelings, feelings of security and happiness within myself and with others.

Before the healing, someone just glancing at their watch would trigger a great rejection. I would believe that that person didn't care about me, and usually this would throw me into deep depression and suicidal thoughts. *NO* deep depression after healing and *NO* suicidal thoughts.

My healing was truly like being "born again," and I definitely feel like my true life didn't really begin until that point of healing.

The Power of the Memory

In prayer for the healing of memories, the power of the memory to make the past present to us in a very real way is extraordinary. The reason for this, of course, is that Jesus, the Infinite One who is outside of time and to whom *all times are present*, enters into what for us is a past occurrence, one known only in retrospect, though we experience its consequences in the present. Here the past-present-future time sequence in which we experience existence comes together in a particularly meaningful way with the Eternal. And that which is eternal within us and therefore not bound by time is sparked. In this way we experience past and present as one—a foretaste perhaps of a way of knowing earth-time we shall one day experience when we are no longer bound by space, mass, and time.

The Holy Spirit's Action in the Healing of Memories

The *essential* action, that which differentiates healing of memories from psychological methodologies, is the action of the Holy Spirit pointing to *the Presence of our Lord who is there*. He has, as it were, walked into that darkest hell of our existence; and even in the midst of the unfolding memory drama, we look with the eyes of our heart (and as so often happens) are enabled to see Him. We receive from Him that healing word, glance, or embrace we've so long needed. We forgive others their darkest sins against us, and He forgives us our sins, and we receive from Him who manifests the very love of God the Father the healing grace we've been unable to receive before. We find out that He was there all along with that healing action, had we only been able to look up and receive it.

Though the Holy Spirit was moving quietly and powerfully to bring psychological wholeness to Lisa, her feeling about herself was far too ugly—her guilt too deep and she too injured—for her to be able to look up and see with the eyes of her heart the Lord in the midst of that hellish memory of her father's sexual abuse, and her mother's violent reaction to it. Much less could she receive the love and healing He had for her. This is as good an example as any of the fact that no two healings are alike, and that healing of memories can never be reduced to a methodology. Rather, it is a matter of the minister's listening to and collaborating with the Spirit. As I listened for the way to break this impasse, I was led to thrust about for just one person in her life through whose love a door might be opened into her heart, one that would enable her to receive His love. I asked her *who* had ever loved her, i.e., who had she ever been able to *receive* love from. It was then that I found out about her aunt.

I then asked the Lord to bring to her memory a particularly wonderful time in which her aunt was present. This happening, I said, "Now crawl up into her lap." As she did this, God's healing moment came. Throwing my arms around Lisa *and her aunt,* I became a sacramental channel through which Jesus' healing love could flow. His love, thus channeled through me and through the remembered love of a long deceased aunt, fully entered in and healed the broken little Lisa.

One of the basic healings here was of what had been to her an utter and absolute rejection by her mother at the time of her father's sexual abuse. This memory, sealed off from conscious awareness, rendered her unable to trust or receive her mother's love, even though her basic psychological need was for a loving relationship with her mother or a mother substitute. In addition, she was then by her aunt's death cut off from the one person whose arms around her at least partially overcame this dreadful deprivation.

I now understood the emotional deprivation behind Lisa's extreme vulnerability and her fall into the hands of the lesbian schoolteacher. As a sexual neurosis, lesbian behavior (except when manifested in an hysterical personality) is not nearly so complicated as male homosexual behavior. Most that I have seen and worked with is rooted in a need for a mother's arms, a need that was never or only insufficiently met. As seen from Lisa's letter, her aunt was the one person whose love Lisa trusted and received. On questioning her, I found that because of this her mother had grown very jealous of this sister, and had finally not allowed her to come to the home. Lisa could then see her only rarely or furtively. But when she did, she was sure to be picked up and clasped tightly in the loving arms of this aunt. "When," I asked, "did you no longer meet with this aunt?" Lisa, thinking about this a moment replied, "She died when I was in the fifth grade." *It was after these embraces were lost to her that she ran into the teacher's arms.* The tragedy for Lisa was that these embraces ended in erotic gestures, and that because she was so terribly starved for a woman's arms and love she failed to fend them off.

Lisa's Identity Crisis

The loss of a mother's love is perhaps the greatest deprivation, humanly speaking, a person can know. The infant comes into the world not knowing itself to be separate from its mother, and it is in her love that it begins to recognize itself as a separate being or person in its own right. In her loving acceptance, the infant son or daughter begins the long and arduous task of emotional and psychological separation from her—one that continues long after it has realized its physical separation from her. Not all lesbian behavior is primarily connected with this early failure to be in a trusting and loving relationship to the mother. But when it is, I've found Lisa's case to be a classic one—one that is illustrative of such cases. In these women I invariably find that there has been for one reason or another[5] this deprivation either in infancy

or early childhood, and this has left each with an awful deficit—
one that she simply cannot make up for until healed of the old
deprivations that have been to her as grievous rejections. She
may or may not recognize *why* she is compulsively drawn toward
women for the affection she craves. It is my experience that she
usually does not.

Healing (wholeness) has to do with mended relationships.

> Christ commanded and empowered his followers to heal, be-
> cause He knew that all men, in their exterior relationships
> and within themselves, are broken and separated. In order
> for man to regain wholeness in every aspect of his life, the
> relationship between himself and God, himself and other
> men, himself and nature, and himself and his innermost
> being, must be healed.[6]

The fallen condition is a crisis in separation, and within the
trauma of broken relationships resides what is described today
as the identity crisis.

When her school counselor sent her for psychiatric care, Lisa
was in the midst of an identity crisis—one that as such had
several levels to it and one that in varying degrees is familiar to
all of us. Hers was especially painful because the circumstances
of her life had almost totally barred her from love, and in large
part therefore from that which partakes of the beautiful and the
true. Evil is, in actual fact, *separation*, separation from that
which completes me. Theologically speaking, sin or evil is
separation from God; psychologically speaking, it is separation
within, and ultimately from my true or higher self:

> We know that the Son of God has come and given us under-
> standing to know him who is real; indeed we are in him who is
> real, since we are in his Son Jesus Christ. This is the true
> God, this is eternal life. My children, be on the watch against
> false gods.[7]

It is significant that the Apostle John here warns of false gods,
for when I am separated from God, I posit my identity in the

creature (the created) rather than the Creator. My eyes will be focused on an idol. But looking to Him, I begin to know who I am. Listening to Him, I begin to die to the old self-centered and self-conscious self. "When all things began, the Word already was,"[8] and He has never stopped speaking. He sends the one word of truth I need, and that word outweighs all the influences of a world that would imprison me in untruth, and separate me from the *Real*. I *hear* what the Word speaks, and the *real me* begins to come forward. Obedient to Him, I begin to experience for the first time what it means to be truly free. With each act of obedience, my will is strengthened and I begin to grow moral fibre; with each act of worship, my spirit is strengthened and I begin to know of a certainty that Another is with me, and lives in me.

Lisa needed, as we all do, healing of the *separations* in her life. She needed release from guilt both false and real, and from the erroneous way in which she in her self-hatred perceived herself. The unhealed memory had militated powerfully against any of these things happening, emitting as it constantly did the nebulous and darkly veiled message, "You are filthy, repulsive, unlovely, and unloveable, and therefore to be rejected." This radiated through the various levels of Lisa's awareness, and out of this came her view of herself. She needed to be brought into the Presence of the Lord, there to be healed of this traumatic memory, there to begin to see herself through His eyes, there to hear His words that—when truly heard—would release her from the dizzying round of negative innuendoes and outright accusations that had long welled up from her wounded heart. Coming into union with Him who not only *heals* but *completes*, she would gain release from self-hatred and fear, and the strength to rise above the limitations the circumstances of her life had placed upon her. Enabled to accept herself, she would then be able to love and accept others.

All of these things the Christian counselor can, in the power of the Spirit, help such as Lisa to do. This is because, according to the words of Jesus, "My Father is always at his work to this very day, and I, too, am working."[9] We learn to see what He is doing and collaborate with Him. We must do these healing works of Christ, this unfettering—for until the Lisas are healed emotionally, they cannot look up to Him in such a way as to receive His love and their unique personhood. Without this, they cannot come into that vital relationship which frees them to relate to all creation and therefore to be all He created them to be.

The Spirit of the Lord is on me; therefore he has anointed me to preach good news to the poor. He has sent me to proclaim freedom for the prisoners and recovery of sight for the blind, to release the oppressed, to proclaim the year of the Lord's favor.[10]

Two

The Causes of Homosexuality: Contemporary Theories

"You might as well face it, Lisa. You are woman-centered; you always have been, you always will be. You need to accept this. You need to accept the fact that you are lesbian and accept that life-style. You were born this way, Lisa. You can't go on fighting it forever."

These words, spoken by one of the two psychiatrists whom she had been under since her junior high school days, rippled like a sickening wave over the bowed head of Lisa. She had just been released from intensive care after her suicide attempt, and was interviewed by him before moving on to her new home in the youth rehabilitation center.

Prayer led us into an understanding of Lisa's condition, and the remedy for it, that is in astonishing contrast to that of the doctors who had cared for her from the beginning. Both had judged her as irremediably lesbian.[1] Whether or not they judged Lisa's so-called lesbian orientation to be constitutional (inborn) or simply irremediable due to a disturbance in her physical or psychological development, I do not know.

What the doctor said to Lisa is all the more shocking when its message sheds its contemporary cloak. He is saying to her, in effect, "Fully find your identity in that one of your own sex you can posit your life and affection in, and do this through genital intimacy."

In heterosexual relationships, the immature woman often attempts to find her life in her mate, and she thereby posits her identity or well-being in him. If she has sexualized her identity (i.e., if she comprehends—at whatever level of awareness, conscious or unconscious—herself as primarily a sexual being), she will attempt to do this principally through genital intimacy. She, like any homosexual lover, will eventually find this a futile as well as degrading exercise. As her own dissatisfaction grows, she will increasingly demand what he does not nor should not have to give. Making him a god, she will be unable to bear the fact that he, like all creatures, has feet of clay. She will get in much the same kind of trouble as those involved in homosexual behavior in that she will never find her true identity through sexual intimacy.

That this intimacy should be the remedy openly touted by the various homosexual apologists and even by many psychologists and doctors as normal and "natural" can only be explained by the fact that sexuality is itself robed in the numinous. It is an idol for sure. Malcolm Muggeridge speaks very plainly to this contemporary condition: "When mortal men try to live without God, they infallibly succumb to megalomania or erotomania, or both. The raised fist or the raised phallus: Nietzsche or D. H. Lawrence. Pascal said this, and the contemporary world bears it out."[2]

Since this book is written primarily as a witness to and illustration of the healing of sexual neuroses through prayer, I do not think it would be especially helpful to analyze to any great extent the current theories about homosexuality. To do that would be to get into all the socio-political ramifications of the problem—those that simply reflect the contemporary mindset; for much of the current rhetoric stems from those quarters rather than from the strictly scientific. Besides, that would be to cover ground already well-tended by others better qualified to write on such subjects.[3] Having said this, I will briefly allude to current views and theories, some of which went into the final "prescription" Lisa's doctor gave her for the alleviation of inner pain and loneliness.

Freud, the father of modern psychoanalysis, viewed homosexuality as a psychological disorder, but believed it to be virtually untreatable. His idea was handed down without adequate refutation until a couple of decades ago. Before Freud and the advent of serious study of the unconscious components of man's behavior, those within the Judeo-Christian tradition, as well as most in the Western world, viewed homosexuality almost exclusively in *moral,* and even to some degree in criminal, terms. As homosexuality began to be studied and eventually understood as one of the most complex of the sexual neuroses, the imbalance tended in the other direction, and many then viewed it almost exclusively in *psychological* terms. In this way, the moral and the spiritual aspects of the problem were laid aside and later denied altogether by some—despite the fact that Freud believed men are at bottom responsible for their choices and therefore for the way in which they attempt to alleviate their inner loneliness and pain.

The average educated person today, brought up in an intellectual climate permeated by popularized and diluted versions of Freudian theory, believes that psychoanalysis states that people are not responsible for their neuroses because these are caused by unconscious complexes, the result of infantile or childhood trauma over which they have no control. This oversimplification, while it contains some truth, does violence to a central aspect of Freud's theory. There is a crucial distinction between *trauma* and *conflict.* In a brilliant article discussing the impact of modern sex research on psychoanalytic thought, Dr. Robert Stoller, a distinguished professor of psychiatry who has specialized in the study and treatment of sexual deviation, explains the difference. Trauma may be in the form of internal sensations, such as hunger or pain; or it may be in the form of external events, such as physical violence or the death of a parent. Such trauma may only cause reaction or change. The affected infant or child may, with more or less pain, automatically adapt to the new circumstances. Dr. Stoller goes on to say that "Not all [traumas] produce conflict; conflict implies intrapsychic struggle in order to *choose* among possibilities." It is conflict, not trauma, which produces an internal fork in the developmental road. The reason this is so important is that neuroses, including perversion of the sexual development, do not result simply from trauma, but from particular resolutions of conflict in this technical sense of that word. As a result of conflict the individual *chooses*, however primitively and unconsciously, one solution over another. [4]

On the heels of this imbalance, that of viewing homosexuality in exclusively psychological terms, came the momentum and attempt to understand homosexuality as a *biological* problem, rather than either a moral or a psychological one. Until fairly recently, the effects of psychological injury in infants before they were able to conceptualize—that is, before, during, and in the first year after birth—were not generally acknowledged. By and large, and for all practical purposes, they still are not understood. To some, therefore, the very early onset of homosexual neuroses appeared to have been constitutional or inborn—to have come with the baby. Attempts to fix the causal factor in the biological did not succeed, however, and in spite of reports to the contrary, there is no real scientific evidence that genetic or endocrine factors are causative in homosexual behavior.

Perhaps for this reason, at the present time homosexual apologists seem to rely most heavily on the theory that homosexual behavior is biologically and psychologically normal—something no more out of the range of normality than that of being born left-handed. Inherent in this idea, of course, is the notion that one is biologically and psychologically determined as either homosexual or heterosexual. Since this has not been established, and in fact flies in the face of all the best biological and psychological knowledge we do have, their arguments quite seriously beg the question. They then go on to rely for the desired effect on association of the homosexual plight with that of the disenfranchised or the minorities everywhere. Their arguments thus rely rather shamelessly on the power of association, and this gimmick is worked to the hilt as their demand for recognition and socio-political power is carefully, if illogically, related to the struggle for equal rights by blacks, women and other minorities.

Some, with a theological turn of mind, and following the lead of an Anglican theologian, have given this argument an added twist with the claim that the homosexual condition is an expression of the variety in creation that God intended. Thus, some voices from within the Church have come to the same conclusion as Lisa's unbelieving psychiatrist and ask, with this added viewpoint to his, "Why—if God made them this way—should their right to genital intimacy be considered immoral?" Some then proceed to invent a system of ethics for this activity that includes faithfulness to one partner and homosexual marriage—in order to avoid homosexual promiscuity! In all this I sense the presence of the phallic god and, in the current exaltation of the instinctual, a bowing down to the dark gods in the blood. Bright Chastity and the joys of Celibacy cannot be talked about in such company. Sweet Reason also hangs her head and exits. I feel a revulsion, not in the presence of one who needs release from the homosexual condition, but in the presence of such trumpeting before a phallic god. The tragic effect of all this, of course, is to bar those like Lisa from the healing they need.

Perhaps these demands from within the Church, outrageous as they are, have done us all a favor. They've pointed quite forcefully to the fact that the Church as a whole has not known how to minister the healing these sufferers need.[5] Therefore, those that hold to the traditional, biblical view concerning both the sinfulness and the healing of homosexuality ("Such *were* some of ye") are looking hard for pastoral answers, and when they do not see them, they cry out, "Where are they?" To cry out for pastoral answers is to cry out for the power to heal the lame in spirit and soul. Homosexual behavior is at once sinful and immature. The sinful aspect has to do with the lameness of the human spirit and is healed through confession and absolution of personal sin. The immature aspect is part of the lameness of the soul—that which is to be set straight so that both spirit and soul can grow into freedom.

If sincerely desired and prayed for, the petition for pastoral answers will bring the Church's healing gifts to the fore. This is what the Rt. Rev. Bennett J. Sims, Episcopal Bishop of Atlanta, has called for in his excellent pastoral statement, "Sex and Homosexuality"[6]: "Out of the conviction that God wills healing, let us hold to the norm of heterosexuality and trust the Spirit's power to make flourish anew the Church's healing gifts."

Three

Matthew's Story: Identity Crisis

Matthew, a darkly handsome, tall and well-built young man, first appeared at my door just after achieving a smashing success in his chosen career. From all appearances this very masculine person had everything going for him: a fine education, a good mind, and a load of talent to go along with his good looks and accomplishments. In spite of all these external appearances and circumstances, however, he was falling apart on the inside. In desperation he had come for help, fearing even to hope that through prayer God could and would ease the inner pain and turmoil and at the same time banish the new thing that had brought every other concern of his life to a head: an onslaught of homosexual feelings for another young man.

Gradually, as I plied him with hot cups of tea, assuring him in the first place that it is easy for God to heal and set right such things, and that in the second place there is really no such thing as being born a homosexual, he relaxed and began for the first time to yield up his painful story. This story involved, of course, that of his parents; and as a Christian, Matthew desired to reveal his parents in the most charitable light. Fidelity to one's parents, even when the parenting has been manifestly bad, is at times a barrier to sharing one's deepest hurts and rejections, and this was so with Matthew. Besides, and even more significantly, he had a feeling deep inside that it was somehow his fault that his parents were unloving. He felt that he was basically unlovable, and that his parents were on that account to be at least partially excused. These feelings had never been verbalized in so many words, but quickly became apparent as he struggled to tell his story.

Matthew's father, the first in his family to be born in the U.S., came of parents who themselves sprang from different language backgrounds and countries. As sometimes is the case with children born into impoverished emigrant families, Matthew's father had known the seamier side of life. He had even been imprisoned for a length of time before Matthew was born and had been treated severely by other prisoners. From the earliest time Matthew could remember, his father was violent of temper and overbearingly authoritarian. He was unreasonable with Matthew, and cruel. His expectations for the boy were often confusing, and could not be lived up to. Matthew never knew quite what would set off his father's temper, at which time there would be beatings and abusive language.

His mother, of yet a different nationality and language background, came to this country as an adult. She proved to be completely defenseless against her husband, both because of her own culture that demanded abject submission to the male, and because of her fearful reaction to his roughshod behavior toward her. She did not speak English very well, and perhaps this partly accounts for the fact that she failed to reach out to others for the support and help she needed to defend herself. Her husband had not wanted children (he had already deserted one family), and she felt guilty for becoming pregnant with Matthew. Just after she gave birth to him, she put him out for adoption; but when no one selected him in the first week, she took him home. The little boy was then a further excuse for her husband to mistreat her. With torn emotions and affections, she was unable to properly mother the boy, and proved to be no bulwark against the unpredictable behavior of the father toward him. The real woman, if she had ever emerged at all, had been ruthlessly ground down. I got the feeling, as Matthew tried to describe his mother to me, of a woman who was almost a non-person. As an adult, he had always felt alienated from her—indeed, not even to know her. Her husband finally divorced her and married another woman. She, helpless, clung rather weakly to her son.

Matthew as a small lad was sensitive and unhappy, and desperately lonely. This loneliness was further heightened through the school years by the fact that his father would not allow his friends to visit in the home. He was, in fact, allowed almost no privileges outside of going to school. One of the things that comforted and diverted him in his growing years was his love for growing things; he loved plants and flowers. One day he planted a garden in the yard, and his father came home in a rage and tore it up. He was deeply crushed. This was one of the most painful memories for which he needed healing.

Matthew had found Christ in his early teen years, and had held to Him like a drowning man. During these teen years, his loneliness and alienation from parents and others continued. He was embarrassed by his mother's inability to speak English properly and her fumbling ways, while at the same time he was ashamed of his lack of good feeling toward her. More than anything else, he yearned for his father's love and hoped always for some word of approbation or encouragement from him, only to find too often the negative or hostile response.

He had done well in his college work and had earned the admiration of his classmates. His personal relationships with men friends suffered, however, as he feared rejection by the very ones he most admired. Girls admired him, but "from afar." His pain and fear of rejection rendered him distant and unknowable in many respects. Those who persevered and pressed through the barrier to get close to the handsome young man realized his deep emotional pain and distress, but did not know how to help him. He struggled with what seemed to him over-powering sexual energies and became fearful of his own sexual drive; he was afraid that he might hurt one of the girls who broke through to him, girls whom he genuinely admired and wanted to know. Mostly he wanted the assurance that they could like him once they knew him, but did not believe this possible.

We come to know ourselves and our place in the love of others in the human family, and ultimately in the love of God. Matthew could not feel himself to be a person of any worth, much less one with the incredible potential of *becoming* rather than simply existing. Believing it impossible that others could ever really love him, he struggled with rootlessness. The truth that God had not only summoned him into the world, but had given him the gift of *place* in it and was calling him to fulfill an exciting artistic and spiritual destiny was a truth totally beyond him at this point.

This, in short, is the story behind what seemed to him to be his major problem: that of strong, homosexual desires toward a man he greatly admired and yearned to have for a friend. These desires were of a frightening intensity; the more he attempted to rationally combat them, the more compulsive they became. He was even dreaming of a homosexual relationship with the young man.

Before we get into what was really happening here, we must look at the overall identity problem he suffered.

Matthew's Identity Crisis

We all have the basic need of being loved and accepted. Matthew had not received the parental love and affirmation he needed to accept his basic identity as a son, loved and cherished by his father and mother. Moreover, he had experienced this rejection even *before* that first week of life when his mother gave him out for adoption. From the moment she was conscious of having conceived him, she feared to give him birth. There was little, if any, cessation of this rejection during the crucial early months of his infancy. To be without love and acceptance at this time is to be in very great need of healing indeed.

Having been insufficiently loved, he therefore could not love and accept himself, and at this point we are into another especially painful level of his identity crisis. Used to harsh words rather than approbation, he had few consoling and affirming words for himself. The memories of painful rejections and hurts from throughout his growing years constantly sent up images and thoughts of himself as something far less than the kind of person he yearned to be—one toward whom the respect and love of others could flow. He listened to the accusing voices from the unhealed psyche and believed them. He hated and rejected himself.

Another level of the crisis concerned that of his sexual identity. Though he possessed the normal sexual drive of a healthy young male, he did not possess the masculine or personal identity to go with it. In lieu of it, a fantasy life sprang into being, one that mirrored dreams he was having at night. Misreading the dreams, he took them to mean that he was homosexual. Before this time compulsive masturbation had been a grievous problem, and one for which he particularly hated himself. It had grown worse instead of better. All the other unhealed identity problems were still with him, underlying this one, participating in it. There was still within Matthew the infant in need of a secure and loving mother, a toddler in need of the love of two parents who could also love one another, a son in desperate need of his father's affirming love and acceptance.

A mother, overly protective and peculiarly or injuriously intimate with a son—unless a strong and affirming father figure is close at hand—can render a son unable to separate his sexual identity from hers, and she thereby becomes part of any propensity toward homosexual behavior that might crop up in him. But Matthew did not have the problem of separating his identity from that of his mother's, as he was all too emotionally and physically remote from her.

Two things in his father's behavior, however, particularly militated against Matthew's coming into a secure sexual identity. First of all, Matthew suffered severely from the lack of a warm and loving father to pattern after, the necessary masculine role model. The loss of an affirming father is a terrible one at any point in the growing years, and this fact is often reflected in prayer for healing in cases outside the context of homosexuality. But these healing sessions convince me that the loss is especially crucial for both boys and girls during and after puberty. As the mother's warm presence and love is so crucial during the first weeks and months of life, so is the father's during adolescence. The finest and most capable mother, try as she may, cannot repair the gap an absent or emotionally remote father leaves on the young teenager. She simply cannot affirm a son or daughter in the way a *whole* father can. This is one of the awful tragedies of divorce and broken homes. There is seldom a father substitute who is both capable and willing to affirm the struggling adolescent boy or girl.

C. S. Lewis has called this period "the dark ages in every life."[1] Few having metamorphosed from narcissistic fledgling to assured man or woman, capable of forgetting self and truly loving others, will venture to argue with him here. Matthew's father, far from helping him to step confidently from this confusing period into his identity as a man among men—one capable of making mature choices, of exercising an assured and benevolent authority over himself and his circumstances, of sexually relating to a wife and fathering children—treated Matthew rather as an appendage or extension of himself, a self he hated. Matthew's inner vision of himself was mainly the one he gained through his father's unaccepting and unloving eyes, a father whose love he yet yearned to win. In yearning for the love and respect of other men, he was at one level looking for his father.

The second aspect of his father's behavior toward him was an even greater threat to the achievement of his masculine identity. He was consistently present to Matthew in a fearful kind of way. His father's hostile and overbearingly authoritarian manner toward his son became the chief instrument behind what I have come to understand and call a severe *suppression of masculinity*.

We are all endowed with a *free* or *active will*. This may be termed the *creative will*, for in contrast to a selfish or self-centered will, it seeks to interact with all that is. I think of the will as a masculine part of our being, whether we are male or female, and it is with this masculine, active will that we responsibly and decisively choose. For instance, in our conversion experience, it is with this will that we choose union and communion with God rather than our own separateness. With it we consciously and deliberately choose the heaven of the integrated and emancipated self rather than the hell of the disintegrated self in separation.[2] This will can be dangerously suppressed, disabled, or even broken entirely. It can simply be overpowered by sloth or *accedia*, termed one of the seven deadly sins because in its full sense it denotes a paralyzed will, a spiritual torpor that in the end constitutes a refusal of all joy. In either case a passive, uncreative suffering results.

The consistently cruel behavior of Matthew's father was a means toward this end in him. As the chances of living to grow a comb are thin for the smallest baby rooster on the tail end of the pecking order, so the chances of Matthew's true masculinity ever coming forward were—apart from God's healing grace—very slim indeed. The overall effect was that of forcing him to put the *real self* to death, that self for whom Christ died that it might freely *become* to the glory of God. Herein we see that true masculinity is bound up with the true self.[3] The emerging, creative masculine person who could love and interact with creation and joyfully plant a garden—or fearlessly and unselfconsciously fall in love with a woman—was the person consistently knocked down.

The Key Insight in Matthew's Case

When Matthew came, breaking under the onslaught of homosexual temptations and dreams, he had no idea of what lay behind them. He could only think of himself as the basest of sinners. How could he, as a Christian, be under such an irrational, powerful, and immoral compulsion? Before we could get into this aspect of his problem, Matthew needed a great deal of prayer for healing of his memories of rejection. He needed to forgive, to be forgiven, and to be released from the effects of his reactions to the sins of others. He needed help in sorting out wrong-headed ideas about God, himself, and others.

By the second session we were ready to deal with the homosexual compulsion, and he was greatly surprised by the following set of questions. In regard to the young man for whom he was experiencing strong homosexual desires I asked him, "What specifically do you admire in this person?" He replied, "His looks, his intellect, the fact that he is successful." These, of course, *were outstanding traits in himself,* but traits that because he could not as yet accept himself, he was denying. I then asked him, "What do you do in your fantasies?" "In my fantasies I want to embrace him, to kiss him on the mouth. I want to come together with him. And in my dreams, that is what I do."[4] After this reply I asked him, "Do you know anything at all about the habits of cannibals? Do you know *why* they eat people?" In utter astonishment he replied, "No, I've no idea why they eat other people." This is a set of questions that are often key in bringing home to such minds and hearts as Matthew's what is really happening in homosexual compulsions. I then told him what a missionary once told me: "Cannibals eat only those they admire, and they eat them *to get their traits."* What was happening to

Matthew was very clear: *he was looking at the other young man and loving a lost part of himself, a part that he could not recognize and accept.*

The first session we'd had together and the resulting prayer for healing of Matthew's painful memories had given me clear insights into both the deprivations he had suffered and the need he had to accept himself. The way was thus paved for this key insight. The strangely idealized vision he had of the young man became increasingly clear. His deep heart knew about this projection, and was revealing the truth in dreams. His "homosexual" dreams that were so frightening to him when taken literally were in effect good messengers sent to say, "Look, you are trying to integrate with a lost part of yourself, but you are going about it the wrong way."

The compelling force behind Matthew's homosexual compulsions was the fact that he was painfully estranged from parts of himself. And several of these parts, consisting of *unaffirmed* and therefore unintegrated attributes of his personality, had played no small part in the professional and artistic success he had just scored. In waking life and in the dream, the young man whom he so ardently admired symbolized these attributes and capabilities of his own personality. Therefore, the way in which we were to pray was at once clear and simple. We would pray specifically that Matthew might be able to recognize, accept, and *come together with* that part of himself he was projecting onto the other young man: the handsome, intellectually keen, and successful Matthew that had never been affirmed by his parents. As we prayed, we would visualize this happening and thus release our faith into a powerful prayer of faith. This one healing prayer would then immediately defuse the power behind the homosexual compulsion.

The Prayer

Once Matthew had gotten a fair understanding of what had been going on inside himself, he was ready and eager for prayer that he might accept those attributes of his own personality he had been projecting onto another. This prayer, as the following weeks proved, did indeed rob the homosexual compulsions of their sting and power.

His immediate need, that of acknowledging those traits vital to his recent success, now identified and ministered to, could no longer plague him by masquerading as a homosexual compulsion. This, however, was only the beginning step in the much larger healing he needed—that of enablement to fully accept himself. He had not known affirmation of himself as a *person*, as a *man*, as a *being of worth*. Within himself were these unaffirmed identities. It was too late for his father and mother to affirm him in a deeply healing and meaningful way, much less for someone else (like myself perhaps) to try to substitute for them. At this point he didn't need a mother or father—he needed to *face the inner loneliness with God*. His full healing would come as he learned to wait, listening, in the Presence of God. In this two-way conversation between himself and God, his full affirmation would come. My part was to invoke the Presence, to call him into it, to see always the real Matthew and appeal only to the man God was calling forth.

Barriers to Inner Healing

There are three major barriers to inner healing and therefore to the maturity and wholeness of personality to which we are called. They are 1) failure to forgive others, 2) failure to receive forgiveness for ourselves, and 3) failure to accept and love ourselves aright. The first two barriers were largely removed for Matthew in the prayer for healing of memories after our first session together. The healing of the traumatic rejections he had suffered had to begin first, because these old wounds were behind his failure to accept himself. He found as we all do, of course, that as more illumination is given, there is more to forgive and for which to be forgiven. His release after our anointing and extensive prayer for this healing was such a soaring and joyful thing that at first he thought he had no further need. But this was the basic healing that would enable him to look upward freely and begin the breathtaking uphill climb from immaturity (freedom from his old inner vision of himself) to maturity with its proper humility and self-acceptance, which is the antithesis to self-centeredness, the wrong kind of self-consciousness and self-love. With this healing he could press on into the freedom to act from the center of his being, that center where Christ dwells and forms the new man, rather than from the locus of the unloved and hurting little boy under the authority of unloving parents and an enigmatic world.

The leveling of this third barrier for Matthew, as in Lisa's case, would require some time, for on the one hand it entailed changing the attitudes and thought-habits of a lifetime. Fr. Michael Scanlon, in his fine book entitled *Inner Healing*, states it this way: "We have an attitudinal life which operates from the very core of our being. . . . This life determines broad general patterns of relating to others and to God."[5] And just as importantly, I would add, *to ourselves.* This is because we cannot love God and others while hating ourselves, while failing to exercise patience and charity toward ourselves. Of this great virtue of patience with the self, the Catholic philosopher Romano Guardini has said, "He who wishes to advance must always begin again. . . . Patience with oneself . . . this is the foundation of all progress."[6]

On the other hand, it entails the "putting on" of Christ and the taking up of the new life. In so doing, every thought of the mind and every picture of the heart is brought into subjection to Christ—a real "practice of the Presence." This is no exercise in abstraction, or even of positive thinking (though it is that and more), but a waiting on Him who is within, without, and all around us, the utter Reality who is capable at any moment of manifesting Himself to the creatures He has fashioned in His own image. Thus we are "made new in mind and spirit, and put on the new nature of God's creating."[7]

Having put Him on, we know that Another is Lord, Another is in charge. Having received Him into ourselves, we know that Another lives through us. The fruits of His indwelling Presence ("love, joy, peace, patience, kindness, goodness, fidelity, gentleness, and self-control"[8]) now issue through us to others, and we who are the channels are healed as well as others in their fragrant wholesome atmosphere. The gifts of this Presence—the power to know, to say, to act—is ours, and we become the masterpiece of harmony God intended us to be. The work of our hands is affirmed. In union and communion with Him, our once fragmented souls are drawn together in one harmonious whole even as the pieces of a complex puzzle fall in place under the guidance of a masterful hand. We are no longer divided within. The psalmist is praying for this healing, I believe, when he cries unto the Lord, "*Unite* my heart to fear thy Name."[9]

The Presence calls forth the true self, up and out of the hell of the false old self, in what can best be described as a resurrection. The true self, with one face, no longer repressed, fearful, or unsteady, shakes off the old pseudo-selves with their myriad faces, and comes boldly forward, gathering all that is valid and real in the personality into itself. We are united within. It is then we can realize the freedom to live out from that center of our being, that place where His Spirit indwells ours, and our will is one with His. We begin to practice not only His presence, but the presence of the new man. We are free from practicing the presence of the old man in whom the principle of death and evil holds sway, and also that of the immature man who is yet under a law (see Galatians 4).

As Matthew well knew, we can be Christians and remain under the law—utterly fail to realize our inheritance and our capacity to walk in the Spirit and practice the presence of the new man. Rather, we practice the presence of the guilty little boy or girl, the "unable to receive the love of God or man" little boy or girl, and are thus rendered unable to exercise the mature authority needed over our own lives or in positions of leadership in the Body of Christ. For this reason too, we cannot move strongly and effectively in the healing gifts of the Spirit. False humility, actual sin, or need for psychological healing bars us from living out from the center, a position of knowing who we are in Him. This position is one of authority, and one by which we the redeemed, even as the unfallen Adam, are *namers* of all that is created. Named by God, and molded by His will alone, we are no longer named and shaped by that which is created. This is the maturity and authority that heals the world. We die daily to any selfish or tyrannical authority (a carnal, dominating spirit) that comes from living out of the self-centered old man, as well as to the weak position of "no authority" of the minor under a law; we live from the center, where He dwells, naming in His name. Our true masculinity is restored. This all creation waits for. All this is involved in the tearing down of the third barrier and of coming into our true identity. It does not happen overnight.

Yet such a healing as this can and does take place so much more quickly than is ordinarily supposed. Often, in contrast to the years of counseling sessions many regularly undergo, two or three weeks will see this healing well underway, depending upon how willing the person is to set aside his own will and learn how to listen to God. Listening prayer is the way to a quick leveling of this third barrier to inner healing. This is a type of prayer all should practice, but often we must be brought to the utterly helpless position of a Matthew or a Lisa before we will give over our servitude to all the other voices within and without and begin to hear and obey the voice of the Good Shepherd. Many of these persons—having suffered breakdowns and long hospitalizations in the past—end up being the strongest and most effective

Christians because, having been under such bondage to the voices of the past and present, they gladly *listen* for the life-giving Word in order to survive as persons.

With the leveling of this third barrier, Matthew found release from his fears of what might happen once his heterosexual identity was fully realized. As a defenseless lad, he had suffered under the unloving tyranny of his father. He was unable to express a right and wholesome anger at the time the emotion was induced, and it was turned inward on himself. Within him, therefore, was not only a suppressed masculinity, but a deeply repressed anger. One could not (and indeed should not) surface apart from the other. But the anger, as well as what seemed to him a fearfully strong sexual drive, left him afraid of his true heterosexual identity. He feared what was inside him and felt he must hold a tight lid on the anger and the sexual drive lest the pent-up energy burst out of bounds. He feared, in short, that he might hurt a physically defenseless woman, treating her as his father had treated him.

As his healing progressed, the anger, as well as the long suppressed masculinity, increasingly made itself known to his conscious mind. Both forces, in fact, began to thunder around inside him like some wild bull elephant storming the bastions of a tropical barricade. Merely attempting to "hold the lid on" was not the answer. He was then ready to find out that all of this could be brought right up out of his heart and into his conversation with God, and that in yielding it to Him it would be transformed.

After learning to do this, he was ready for what had seemed to him a very risky prayer—the prayer for release of his normal heterosexual drive. As an example, I would like to share Agnes Sanford's wonderful way of prayer for this. She images the dormant or misguided sexual energy within a person as a "creative flow."

You see, what we call sex is only a part of the whole creative flow of God's life within us. So I think of God's life in us like a river that perhaps has been dammed up at some point. At any rate, for some reason it has overflowed its banks, has come into an area where it does not belong.

Because the words "love" and "sex" are heavily loaded with differing emotional and sensual connotations, especially to someone with a sexual problem, Mrs. Sanford avoids using them in her prayer. She speaks instead of "the flow of creative life from God" and of "the life of Jesus Christ coming in." For a like reason, she purposely speaks impersonally and even, she says, "almost coldly" throughout the prayer.

And so I lay hands on this person . . . then I pray for His life coming in to look at this river and bring it right back to its normal channel. I do this very pictorially, and sometimes I say, "Now by faith I dig the channel deep and wide. In the Name of Jesus Christ I say that this creative energy from now on shall flow in its normal channel, and it shall not overflow anymore to the right hand or to the left hand. I build high dikes on the right hand and on the left hand and in Jesus' Name I command that it shall not overflow to the left hand or the right hand, but it shall flow quietly in its normal channel." If the person is married, which they sometimes are, I say "finding sufficient release in the normal acts and joys of married life." If the person is not married I say "finding sufficient release for the present in physical exercise, in creative activity, mental interests, and let any excess of this feeling now be lifted, shifted, sublimated, and transformed into Agape, into the compassion of God that goes forth to heal men, women or children regardless."

Agnes, though speaking to God, is praying in a picture language that the sufferer's deep mind can grasp. In this way her prayer does not lay a burden on his beleaguered conscious mind. She knows only too well that

This person cannot cope with this difficulty in the conscious mind. . . . No use reasoning and arguing and beating your breast. . . . The more he worries about it, the worse it gets. I always tell the man, don't even pray about it; you can't do that; it will be done for you; you just leave it alone.

During this prayer, however, the faith that bypasses the conscious mind is released as the person "sees" with the eyes of his heart a symbolic picture of his own healing, and begins to participate from this deep level in the prayer. There is no better way to release a prayer of faith than this. [10]

Agnes, her arms in motion to demonstrate this pictorial prayer, sets this misguided river of energy into its right channel:

It's not hard. It's an easy kind of prayer. Just kind of lift it up a bit—there it is, you see, it's God's flow of creativity. It has just overflowed. Bring it back, lift it up. [11]

For Matthew, as for others, the timing of this prayer is important. For instance, God had other work to do in Matthew's soul before he was ready for this. Even so, I have to agree with Matthew that it *is* a risky kind of prayer because, when prayed in its proper sequence, it always (as Agnes says) works! Therefore, in praying such a prayer as this for Matthew or anyone else, I emphasize quite heartily the "finding sufficient release for the present in physical exercise," etc. God delights in answering specific prayers. He readily heard and answered on Matthew's behalf.

More about the Failure to Accept Ourselves

Within this third barrier to inner healing lies a failure to negotiate what is at one level a perfectly natural developmental step common to all men everywhere. There are, as the psychologists point out, progressions from infancy to maturity which involve steps of "psycho-social development." When we miss one of these normal progressions, we are in trouble.

One of the progressions vital to this matter of self-acceptance is the step *from* the narcissistic period of puberty, that "auto-erotic," self-centered phase when one's attention is more or less painfully centered on one's own body and self, *to* that developmental level whereby one has accepted himself and has turned his eyes and heart outward toward all else in the created world. To whatever degree one fails in regard to this step, he will find himself stuck in some form or manifestation of the wrong kind of self-love. Failing to love himself aright, he will love himself amiss. The rampant morbid practice of introspection, for example, is one of the most prevalent of these manifestations, and the anxious practice of it can be as pernicious to personality development as that of masturbation (when carried past puberty) and homosexuality—two of the more obvious examples of a love turned inward.

There are, of course, a multitude of ways in which we can love the self to the exclusion of others. I remember only too well the young wife who realized her husband's narcissism in his very act of lovemaking. She said to me, "My husband is in love with his own body. I am most aware of this when he is making love to me. He doesn't really—can't really—make love to me, though I can hardly explain it to you. I have seen him nude, gesturing before a mirror. He gets the same pleasure out of that as in making love to me. I am not loved. I am merely a vessel through whom he loves himself." This man sorely needed the healing we are here talking about. In meeting with him later I found that he suffered fits of black depression in which he despised himself. He needed freedom from a narcissistic love the flipside of which was a nonacceptance and even hatred of the self.

To write about the healing of the homosexual is to write about the healing of all men, for every one of us has been stuck in some diseased form of self-love. Indeed, that is what the Fall in every individual life *is*. Christ not only redeems us from the effects of the Fall, but continues to free us as we come regularly before Him repenting the pride that continues so quickly and easily to beset us. Always, in order to keep whole, we must continue to confess pride, that root of all darkness, the self-serving kind of love.

Walter Trobisch has written on the need for self-acceptance in a booklet entitled *Love Yourself*. In it he states simply and truthfully two facts that I see borne out continually in respect to the right kind of self-love. First,

> It is an established fact that nobody is born with the ability to love himself. [12]

He then quotes the German psychotherapist Dr. Guido Groeger:

> Self-love is either acquired or it is nonexistent. The one who does not acquire it or who acquires it insufficiently either is not able to love others at all or to love them only insufficiently. The same would be true for such a person in his relationship to God. [13]

Second, Walter Trobisch states:

> To put it bluntly, *Whoever does not love himself is an egoist.* He must become an egoist necessarily because he is not sure of his identity and is therefore always trying to find himself. Like Narcissus, being engrossed with himself, he becomes self-centered. [14]

An example of self-love in the negative sense is illustrated by the Greek myth about Narcissus. He was a youth who, while gazing at his reflection in a well, fell in love with himself. Totally engrossed with his own image, he tumbled into the water and drowned. From this myth, the word *narcissism* is derived. Another Greek term for "self" and "love" denoting the same idea is *auto-eroticism.*

Self-love used in the positive sense of self-acceptance is the exact opposite of narcissism or auto-eroticism. It is actually a prerequisite for a step in the direction of self-lessness. We cannot give what we do not possess. Only when we have accepted ourselves can we become truly self-less and free from ourselves. If, however, we have not found ourselves and discovered our own identity, then we must continually search for ourselves. The word *self-centered* aptly describes us when we revolve only around ourselves.[15]

The failure to pass from the narcissistic stage on into that of self-acceptance is what we are here calling the third barrier to inner healing, the failure to accept and love oneself aright. I have written at some length on this matter because of the fact, greatly impressed on me as I studied the data of each healing, that this failure is common to each one, no matter what category of homosexuality his or her story fits in. A study of homosexuality turns out to be a study of arrested growth in at least a part of the personality; it is a study in immaturity. Indeed, as reiterated throughout this book, it is a study in both the psychological and spiritual aspects of the identity crisis.

Equally as thought-provoking to me has been the importance of the father's role during, and in the formative years just after, puberty. It appears to be crucial to the young son or daughter's negotiation of this "psycho-social developmental step."[16] The father's affirmation of his young one has been indispensable all along, of course, laying as it does the groundwork for a trusting relationship later on. But he must not opt out at this critical time in the life of the adolescent. The fact that the father's loving and affirming presence (or that of an extraordinary father substitute) is the ladder by which the young son or daughter takes this crucial developmental step up to self-acceptance has been impressed on me over and over again. This calls for a reasonably whole father, one who has himself made the step. His part is then the crucial one, even as the mother's was during the first months of life, from conception to the child's realization that it is a separate entity from her. There is never a time in a child's life when it does not need the love of a whole father and a whole mother, but apparently some stages are more critical than others for psychological health and development.

It is one of the tragedies of our culture that fewer and fewer of us move from puberty on into this step. We remain in various arrested states below that of a serene self-acceptance, with its release from the mood swings between a selfish egoism on the one hand and an annihilating self-hatred on the other. Thus we are slaves to our own emotional beings, and we live precariously out from the locus of our own feeling beings. This we do until the pain of having missed this developmental step grows so intense that we begin to awaken from our stupor, and begin the search for wholeness. Many, never finding answers and healing, go to their graves never having stepped across the line from immaturity to maturity. The main reasons for this cultural impasse are not hard to find. The father is simply more often than not unavailable to his adolescent son or daughter. This may be by reason of divorce or simply because no time is left over from business or profession. Often the father's own self-serving manner of life and immaturity render him unable to affirm his son or daughter. Or it may even be that our permissive society has prematurely freed the son or daughter from the father's rightful authority. Much of the homosexuality we see today is the harvest sown by the breakup of the American home and the absence of whole and affirming fathers.

Another Prayer Matthew Needed

Another specific prayer Matthew needed was for release from the habit of masturbation. I have yet to pray for healing of the homosexual condition in a male without finding the necessity to pray also for the release from this habit. A fantasy life may or may not accompany it and thus have to be dealt with.

Masturbation is often a feature of puberty; as the narcissistic period lingers, so does the habit. Sometimes this narcissistic habit has even been a root factor leading to a homosexual lifestyle, as will be seen in a later case.

In some instances, however, the habit is rooted in infantile trauma and is related to severe dread and anxiety—those components accompanying the severest psychological injuries in infants. In these cases, a dread-ridden masturbation (rather than a merely lustful one) ensues. The infant, unable to receive the love of the mother or someone other than himself, will anxiously clutch at his own genitals. Dr. Frank Lake, Christian psychiatrist and depth-psychologist, states that infantile dread manifests itself as painful genital tension. He quotes Kierkegaard who noted that with an increase of dread, there is an increase of sensuality. This is the pain and dread of being *dis-related*, first of all as an infant to its mother. In this separation, the infant can fail to achieve a sense of well-being or even of being at all.[17]

There are differing degrees of the damage here, but in cases where dread and anxiety are a factor, the counselor must help the sufferer not only to be released from the habit, but to exercise patience and understanding with himself while the underlying anxiety and identity crisis is being healed. And it will always be healed as the person comes into his identity and relationship in Christ. Also, even though there is a pathological base to the habit, the sufferer who truly desires wholeness must consciously turn from it. The habit always contributes to self-revulsion and self-hatred, and will be found rankling at the bottom of a continuing bad self-image until the necessary freedom is gained. The habit thereby stands in the way of overcoming that third big barrier to inner healing: that of coming to accept and love oneself aright.

Such a sufferer needs to understand what such a dread-ridden cycle of masturbation denotes: a love turned inward on oneself due to his primary dis-relation to others. And also, he needs to know that the continuing habit, as a love mistakenly turned inward, militates against his coming into right relationships with others. Though these persons need guilt removed rather than added to, it is my experience to see them healed all the more quickly as they ask forgiveness for this wrong kind of self-love, while at the same time they learn the great virtue of patience with themselves, and the ability to forgive themselves if and when they fall.

Illumination as to the why of such a habit is in itself healing. I ministered to a young man who had throughout his life suffered shame and been unable to accept himself due to his anxious and dread-ridden bouts with compulsive masturbation. He was from a devout Catholic home, and so the guilt he felt was all the more intense. His mother, seeking help for him, had become a prayer group leader and in that capacity attended a School of Pastoral Care. There she heard me say that some of the most remarkable healings I see have to do with the healings of rejections one has experienced *before* birth, and this brought her son's need forcefully to mind. Though he was greatly loved, due to the circumstances of her life at the time she became pregnant with him, she had grievously rejected the unborn infant. The mother of nine children, she had broken in health of mind and body at the time of her seventh pregnancy. Feeling herself incapable of bearing another child, she began to sink in anger and frustration at her plight. A dreadful loneliness swept over her, one that her husband was unable to enter into and lift from her. All this had brought the family closer to God and to each other, but not before she had attempted suicide as a way out. By the time of her son's birth, though still suffering from nervous exhaustion, she was enabled to lovingly receive and nurse her little son.

As a small child and throughout his growing years he had required special attention, including psychiatric care. When he came to see me at his mother's urging, he knew nothing of his mother's severe disappointment in finding herself pregnant with him. He thought himself to be simply lustful and grievously oversexed, a thing that caused him to fear his sexual drive and his longing to marry. After he had shared with me the strivings in his life to overcome self-hatred and the terrible lifelong problem of masturbation, we went to prayer.

Almost immediately we were into a "trauma of birth" healing. He was being born and was engulfed by a dread-filled loneliness. It seemed we stayed in that memory an unusually long time, but the rejection he had experienced had been very deep. Over and over again, his voice full of anxiety and dread, he described what he was experiencing at birth: "I am so lonely, so alone." We invited the Lord into the midst of that truly awful loneliness, and asked Him to hold the little infant tightly to His breast. We waited in His Presence until the young man was healed. His lifetime battle against clutching at his genitals when anxious and lonely was won.

Matthew's habit, like this young man's, was not simply a hangover from childhood sex-play or the narcissistic period of puberty, but was born of infantile dread and anxiety. It had been with him since he could remember, and had to do with the pain of being separated from loving relationships—of being dis-related. It was as he came to accept himself in the affirming love of God and of his brothers and sisters in Christ that he won his freedom from this compulsive, anxiety-ridden habit.

As often is the case, however, lust had somewhere along the line entered in.[18] Besides needing prayer for healing of the habit as it related to anxiety and dread, Matthew needed a prayer for deliverance from lust. This put to flight a spirit of sex (sexual lust) that had taken occasion by his need for inner healing to work an additional bondage of lust in him. As always in the case of a lust, a radical choice must be made before such a prayer as this. Matthew had to choose never to allow admission to that lust, along with its fantasy life, into his mind again.

It is perfectly amazing how often, even in the severest cases of psychological distress, the sufferer finds it difficult to make this choice. One unforgettable picture of this hesitation is that of the ghostlike man in C. S. Lewis's *The Great Divorce*. He stands outside of Heaven trying to hang on to a little red lizard of lust who lives on his shoulder, and whispers in his ear, refusing ever to be quiet. An Angelic Spirit, aflame with light, stands before him, inviting him to choose Heaven and joy. The little red lizard of course stands in the way of this choice and has got to go. When the Angel offers to kill it, the Ghost cries out, "You didn't say anything about *killing* him at first. I hardly meant to bother you with anything so drastic as that."[20] He then desires a gradual release, but is assured by the Angel that *that* method does not work at all. Finally, screaming to God for help, the Ghost allows the Angel to kill it.

> The Burning One closed his crimson grip on the reptile: twisted it, while it bit and writhed, and then flung it, broken backed, on the turf.[21]

The Ghost begins to turn into an immense, golden-headed man, not much smaller than the angel, and the lizard metamorphoses into a great silvery white stallion with mane and tail of gold. The metamorphosis, so wonderfully meaningful, pictures the beautiful reality for which the revolting little lizard of lust has been the substitute. A lustful habit, with its accompanying fantasy life, threatens not only the spiritual life of the Christian, but the true imagination as well.[22] It effectively withholds from sight the powerful silver-and-gold stallion.

Matthew chose joy over lust, and by prayer we put the red lizard to flight.

Then and Now

Several years passed after Matthew first appeared at my door; and, as a gracious Providence would have it, he returned to fill my doorway again with his good-looking—and this time, joyfully vibrant—presence. It was a different doorway and in another state, as we both now hail from different parts of the country. But once again, only in a more festive manner, we talked over steaming cups of tea in my living room.

Matthew has come so far from the quiet desperation he once knew that it almost seems never to have been. Indeed, I hated to remind him of it by asking him to read and comment on his own story before it went into print. His own parents have grown and changed a great deal for the better because he has been able to love and direct them in straighter and more fulfilling paths. He likes to think of them as they are now.

Also, from having little sense of his identity as a person in his own right, as a son in a family, and as a man among men, Matthew now rests easily in an increasingly secure knowledge of who he is, and of loving acceptance by others. I think one of the most notable changes in his outward personality is his delightful sense of *becoming*. He knows *joy* in the knowledge that with God he is indeed fulfilling an exciting spiritual and artistic destiny. With this has come a growing sense of *place*. That God has both summoned him into the world and given him the enormous gift of place in it is yet for him a thing to marvel over.

Along with increasing success in his chosen profession is a growing ministry to others he meets along the way. Those suffering from the problems he once knew seem to gravitate toward him. He has been amazed to find himself a channel of God's healing to others who suffer under the very problems he once thought there was no help for.

Matthew is one whose "homosexuality" was never acted out, but most certainly would have been had he not received the psychological healing he needed. His inner orientation was severely slanted in that direction, and had he succeeded in acting out his deeply rooted fantasy life, his healing would have taken longer. Of all this no one is more aware than he, and his exclamation, "Truly God has always had his hand on me!" is one of awe and thanks to God, who not only kept him from falling, but has preserved him from the time of infancy. He knows beyond all shadow of a doubt that if God could and would heal him, He can and will heal anyone. He knows also that there is really no such thing as a "homosexual" person. There are only those who need healing of old rejections and deprivations, deliverance from the wrong kind of self-love and the actions that issue from it, and—along with that—the knowledge of their own higher selves in Christ.

Four

The Search for Sexual Identity

Sexuality and sexual behavior are dimensions of humanness, but they do not constitute a person as a human being—Bennett J. Sims, Bishop of Atlanta

The accounts of Lisa's and Matthew's *healings* reveal the sexual identity crisis in the only context in which it is to be understood—that of the overall search for identity and personhood. The truth that wholeness (healing) has to do with mended relationships (between oneself and God, oneself and others, and oneself and one's innermost being) has, I trust, been adequately pointed up and emphasized. The stories of Lisa and Matthew were selected because both knew extremes in the trauma of *separation*. The tales of their lives provide classical examples of conditions, and reactions to those conditions, that can lead a woman to be inordinately woman-centered, a man to be inordinately man-centered. The individual may *choose* a lesbian or homosexual relationship when the need for intimacy becomes compulsive. This choice is made as a way to alleviate the inner loneliness and in an attempt to find a sense of identity in relationship to another.

The following stories of crises in sexual identity are related in brief to point out other frequent variations and patterns in homosexual behavior. From our Lord's ministry, we can see that no two healings are ever the same, and therefore prayers for healing can never be reduced to mere formulas or methods. But in prayers with persons who fear that they may be homosexual, and with those involved in homosexual behavior—whether overt or in the fantasy life—I've come to recognize certain root problems and basic psychological needs. These fall into discernible groups, along with the ways to pray about them. These groupings overlap, and some stories would fall into one or more of them.

Suppressed Masculinity

Stan's Story

Stan's dilemma was chiefly due to the smallness of his person. Because of his anguish over this, he had doubts and fears about his sexual capabilities. These anxieties grew as he continued to reject his small body, and with it his own masculinity. As a college senior and long past the period of puberty, he had as yet failed to accept himself and go on from there to gain a secure sexual identity. This problem became critical when he, like Matthew, found himself enmeshed by compulsive homosexual fantasies.

These started with unbidden mental images which assaulted his mind when he would see other fellows in gym showers. Invariably these images would concern the athletic types. Stan, unlike Matthew, did not admire the intellect and the good looks of another, but the physical size and athletic prowess that characterizes the All-American athlete. To his current state of mind, these were the characteristics essential to sexual virility. The unbidden imagery darting in and out of Stan's mind therefore centered on the genitals of the male he admired. And here again we recognize the analogy between the homosexual compulsion and the cannibal's reason for eating a fellow human—in order to get his good traits. Both reflect a twisted way we try to take into ourselves those attributes we feel we are missing.

An unbidden and recurring mental image that suddenly assails the mind, when it is *entertained subjectively,* becomes part of an ongoing compulsive fantasy in that person's life. On the other hand, when it is immediately *objectified*—that is, held outside oneself (so to speak) and analyzed—one not only can begin to read its psychological implications, but take authority over it. Whether it is a symbolic picture welling up from an unhealed psyche, or a destructive missile from the enemy of our souls, it can be discerned through prayer and thereby utterly disarmed. Often, and that is the burden of this book, it is both these things working together, and we must take care to pray for the healing of the psychological factor as well as that of the spiritual. In this way we discern between the need for healing of the soul and its protection and deliverance from the alien forces that would oppress and lie to it. Satan, both tempter and accuser (Revelation 12:10), takes full advantage of a person's psychological problem (in Stan's case, his failure to secure his sexual identity).

Stan lost the battle in this onslaught against the mind by allowing lust to enter in. More than a little influenced by the current homosexual propaganda and having failed to secure his sexual identity, he began subjectively to entertain, rather than objectify and take authority over, the phallic images that plagued his mind. In this way he opened himself to temptation and, finally, to a moral and spiritual fall that ended in overt homosexual acts.

Had Stan gotten the help he needed before falling into overt homosexual behavior, he would have spared himself intense suffering, for he very quickly came under severe demonic oppression. He had always been a very sensitive, moral person, and had won honors for academic and artistic excellence in a university noted for both. His mind, however, was now held captive not only by a demonic imagery, but by a vicious and continuous mental obsession that contained two elements: a constant analyzing of himself, an exercise in which he was continually looking inward to find some sort of a personal truth or reality, and a constant analyzing of what he had before accepted as true. This inner dialogue was full of an irrational sophistry that could only tear concepts apart, but could never put the fragments back together in any kind of satisfying whole. Another way to describe this is to say that his thought, severely introspective and full of doubts about what is or is not true, was agonizingly painful and circular. This is the disease of introspection,[1] and Stan had it to a fearful degree. He was in fact floundering in serious mental and spiritual darkness and was filled with fear when he first sought help through prayer.

Our first prayer was one in which I commanded the powers of darkness to release his mind and depart from him. I use Holy Water (water blessed and prayed over by a priest and set apart for this purpose) in such a prayer so as always to have the prayers of the Church united with mine. It is one of the simplest and quickest prayers we are privileged to pray, and only requires that we know and move in the authority given to us as Christians. The Holy Spirit's gift of discerning of spirits is in operation *before* such a prayer is made.[2] The relief this prayer brings, once the demonic is truly discerned and sent away, is immediate.

The next prayer for Stan was with anointing of oil[3] for the healing and quieting of the mind. Under the Holy Spirit's leading, we pray according to that person's individual need. Usually in a case like this, however, I anoint the forehead with oil, making the sign of the cross on the forehead. Then, laying my hands on the head (or sometimes gently pressing both temples), I ask Jesus to enter in, and to heal and quiet the mind. I wait, quietly praying, *seeing* Him do this very thing. After this prayer, Stan was ready to make his confession and receive the needed cleansing and forgiveness.

After this we had to tackle his psychological need, that of accepting himself as small, and of accepting his masculinity even though it came in a smaller frame than he had heretofore been able to accept. Ideally, as we have pointed out in Matthew's case, this step should have been taken just after puberty and long before this time. It was yet a formidable leap for him, and he needed sensitive love, wisdom, and affirmation from one who would wait and listen to the Lord with him until such time as he could make the hurdle safely.

This is, as we have seen, an attitudinal block which we overcome as we deliberately *choose* to forsake our old unaccepting and unloving attitudes toward the self and bring the thoughts of the mind and the imaginations of the heart (in this case, all the old negative thoughts and imaginations about oneself) into subjection to Christ (2 Corinthians 10:5). We then begin to see ourselves, not through our own eyes or even the eyes of others, but through His loving, accepting eyes. We are thus instilled with, and learn to exercise, the virtue of patience and gentleness toward ourselves as well as others. It is on our knees—or however we best get into a two-way conversation with God—that we consciously and deliberately accept ourselves, and begin the task of *listening,* of becoming present to our own hearts as well as to the heart of God.

Particularly humiliating memories from the past can make us afraid to listen to God and to our own inner selves and feelings, for fear of what we might find when we do. Some of us fear that when we really face the truth about ourselves, we will know for sure that our worst fears are in fact true—that we are somehow viler than others, or perhaps less "normal" than everyone else we know. We run then from facing our inner loneliness and are terrified of either solitude on the one hand, or of the satisfying intimacy and companionship we need with our friends and family on the other. But all who take their courage in hand and enter into this kind of prayer, no longer fearing to see and acknowledge before Him either the ignoble things in their past or their deep inner feelings about themselves *and others*, are the ones who find that God is truly love. They also find the virtue (a gift from God) of self-acceptance.

For Stan, even after he had accepted God's forgiveness, the *fact* that he *had fallen* in such a way held him back from accepting himself and therefore from the goal of freedom and maturity. Besides forgiving himself, he had to be patient and gentle toward the self that had erred, and reject only the sinful behavior. Stan had to realize that a failure to do this could only be rooted in pride.

This is the pride that until realized and confessed bars us from coming to terms with the fact that we are, like everyone else, fallen creatures, and therefore are sinful and do make grievous mistakes. This failure is usually hiding under what we term an "inferiority complex," something that always involves a form of pride lurking within. We are yet trying to work out our own salvation. In confessing our pride, we acknowledge that we are like all other men—fallen and prone to the vile as well as to the beautiful, and that if we turn from Him but for a moment we are once again capable of the shameful and the sordid. This is the full acceptance of the way of the cross—God's way of saving us which bypasses our attempts to win salvation for having been perfect, or having figured out a way to "undo" our past sins and mistakes.

Usually, once this great truth of free and "amazing grace" is understood, a person can go on to settle the matter of self-acceptance by himself. This ordinarily takes a good bit of "wrestling" in prayer against our old attitudes, but that is what makes us strong. In cases where the diseased emotional view toward the self is particularly difficult and of long standing, however, more help is needed. With these persons, my part is simply to wait with them in prayer, gently directing them to let go of their negative ideas, and receive in their place the positive words and attitudes the Lord sends. Sometimes, in particularly difficult cases, we go back into the memories that have already been healed through prayer. This time, however, the person is consciously and deliberately, in conversation with the Lord, to *accept* the self who has participated in the hated behavior and take care to reject only the harmful behavior.

In this way, those who are so rejecting of themselves can gain the necessary objectivity they need to exercise the same patient acceptance of themselves as they would toward another person. This is, at the same time, a deeply meaningful lesson in a proper humility, the kind that humbly accepts the penitent and forgiven self. It frees those like Stan from the depression their anger toward themselves has generated. This kind of prayer defuses, deflects, and indeed entirely disperses the anger. Thus humbled before Him, they are enabled to accept themselves, and He lifts them up and makes their lives meaningful.[4]

This listening prayer is the best possible training in the practice of the Presence of God. In looking to Him, we are drawn up and out of the hell of self-consciousness and introspection. We become God-conscious. Stan learned resolutely to check himself when he was turning inward—the practice of the presence of self—and, in that very moment, to cast his mind and the eyes of his heart (imagination) on the Lord. "I will keep him in perfect peace whose mind is stayed on Me,"[5] has always been the promise of God, and it is the very best way of all to be healed of the disease of introspection.

In this *listening prayer* new light is shed on one's past, and we gather insight into the *whys* of our particular weaknesses. Stan, himself a perfectionist, began to realize that in this he reflected his father's perfectionism. Along with this, he saw that two basic attitudinal patterns had evolved in himself: 1) the pattern of not wanting to displease, and 2) the pattern of being subservient to his mother through fear of displeasing her. He saw that he had tried to protect his mother in this way, and why he had done so. His brother, a year or so older, had been unmanageable, and his mother, attributing this to the fact of his sex, prayed and prayed that the next baby would be a girl. Instead of the girl, Stan arrived, and he somehow realized his mother's fear of having another difficult son. From as far back as he could remember, he tried to be perfect. He tried to fulfill all her expectations as to what a good baby and a good son would be. In later deference to her, he did not attempt to establish the usual boy-girl relationships. All this came as new insight to Stan and was the fruit of his exchanging the old habit of introspection for the discipline of listening prayer.

These personal circumstances, of course, did not prepare him for the work of separating his identity (sexual and otherwise) from that of his mother, but there was an even more important factor in this difficulty. His father, though a very fine man, was deeply engrossed in his work and was also emotionally remote from his son. Stan, an intensely loyal person, could hardly admit that he barely knew his father, though he had placed him high on a pedestal. He therefore did not have the necessary relationship with his father during the crucial years of puberty and immediately after, that time when he so desperately needed paternal affirmation in order to emerge from the narcissistic cocoon of adolescence and accept his mature masculine identity.

To listen is to obey. In learning obedience, one's true self—masculinity and all—comes forward. As Stan made his will one with Christ's he found and accepted his full masculine identity. It was there all the time—waiting for him. He did not win it without a struggle, but in the struggle was the full metamorphosis. Like the butterfly moth, he grew very strong and brightly colored wings with which to fly and explore the universe. He is a sturdy, stable person now, one who is amiable, content, and in possession of his heterosexual identity. His academic and artistic talents have blossomed and at the time of this writing are earning him extraordinary success.

I believe one of the strong demonic intentions was to bereave him of his unusually fine artistic and intellectual talent. Another factor bears mentioning, one that left him all the more open to such a serious assault on his mind. In lieu of having accepted himself, Stan totally immersed himself in intellectual and artistic pursuits, and neglected the spiritual, physical, and emotional parts of his being. We are more vulnerable to temptations and odd compulsions when we develop one part of the mind or personality at the expense of another.

Jay's Story

Jay came from a Christian home, one with an abundance of love and affection. He had, however, a very weak father (whom he and his mother loved and accepted just as he was) and a very dominant mother, one who early in his life had a penchant for dressing him as a little girl. One of his earliest memories was that of being dressed in a pink frilly dress by his mother, who then invited several members of her family in to admire him. This was apparently the mother's way of adjusting to the fact that she had wanted a girl and had given birth to a boy instead. Understandably enough, there had been a conflict of feeling in the family at the sight of Jay in pink ruffles, and this had impressed the event on his mind along with the emotions it had stirred up. Oddly enough, he had not thought his mother blameworthy in this, and it was evident that he loved her dearly. As I was to find out, he had modeled himself after her—had imitated *her* movements and actions rather than those of his father.

Jay was a senior in high school when he first realized he needed some help his mother could not give him. He enjoyed acting in his school's drama productions, and had just won the masculine lead role in a tender and beautiful story of young love. Instead of being happy, he found himself in turmoil. He did not want to play the part of the virile prince. He wanted, in the keenest kind of way, to play the part of the soft, feminine beauty whom the prince rescues and marries. This was a terrible discovery, one that awakened him to sudden fears about himself. These fears were compounded when about this same time several of his peers began to suggest he was homosexual, and would point to his mannerisms as proof.

Since Jay had modeled after his mother, his mannerisms (walk, talk, movement of the hands) were decidedly feminine. Also, due to this patterning and the closeness of their relationship, he was slow in separating his sexual identity from hers. Because of this, his masculine characteristics were underdeveloped, his feminine characteristics fully developed. Also due to this, even though he enjoyed good and close relationships with girl friends, he did not have the usual problems of reining in or curbing the sexual drive common to most boys his age.

The first thing Jay needed, after assurance that he was not homosexual, was the fullest realization of *what* had happened to him—i.e., that he had modeled himself after his mother instead of his father. He also needed illumination as to *why* this had happened. We were then ready to pray for healing of those memories that had contributed to his sexual identity confusion.

Strangely enough, he had to be convinced of his need to forgive his mother for 1) wanting a girl instead of a boy, and 2) for dressing him as a little girl—for as he repeatedly declared, he held nothing against her. I had to impress upon him the fact that though he happily bore her no resentment, he needed to *take exception* to her actions in regard to him and forgive her for them.

As we began to pray, the first memory that came up was the one of him as a baby in pink frills surrounded by frowning relatives. As the Lord moved into this memory, and as he forgave his mother (he had heretofore identified with her feelings rather than those of the displeased relatives), he seemed to see his mother's actions in a truer light for the first time. One by one, instances of his mother's treating him as a girl came up for him to "see" and deal with. He began to understand how her actions had affected his ideal image of himself, and that he had to change that image insofar as it excluded his masculinity. It was no small task to deliberately imagine a different ideal image of himself than that one which his mother had praised and affirmed.

It was important also that he give thanks to God for his mother's love and affection, and that he reject *only* her mistaken and misguided behavior toward him as a male. This was very easy for him to do as their relationship was on the whole a good and loving one. It was made even easier when he realized she too needed healing. Her father had wanted a boy when she was born, and she had experienced a deep rejection. To exacerbate the problem, she had been given a man's name.

After we had prayed about these matters, I anointed his forehead with oil and asked our Lord to enter in, to heal and to set in their normal course the sexual desires and drives of the seventeen-year-old Jay. We pictured this healing taking place, and thanked God for it.

After this prayer I directed him to consciously and deliberately change his mannerisms, and suggested that he select the most masculine man he could think of to model after—one he admired as a Christian, a leader, a husband, and a father—and this he promised to do.

Jay, excited about all the new light on what had been a very painful dilemma and greatly encouraged by the prayers, left my home and I did not hear from him for four or five months. He then rang up for a second appointment.

When he arrived, I was more than a little amazed at the improvement in his mannerisms. One would have to look very close to find even a hint of his old mannerisms in speech or movement; his acting ability undoubtedly helped him achieve such a change in so short a time. And his problem this time was altogether different. His masculinity was no longer suppressed, his sexual identity was separated from that of his mother's, and he had experienced the release and normalization of the sexual drive. He was, however, having trouble because his sexual desires and drives, no longer repressed, seemed excessive.

There was a way to pray for this problem too. We thanked God for this creative energy within Jay, and asked that any excess might be channeled through exercise and other creative activity until such a time as he married.

Before leaving Jay's story, I need to point out the tragic results that can come about through suggesting or accusing someone of being homosexual because his appearance or actions suggest the opposite sex. Before someone like Jay is illuminated as to *why* he appears effeminate,[6] such a suggestion or accusation comes across with what I can only describe as supernatural force. It is as though Satan himself takes up the accusation, convinces the victim that what is untrue is true, and then turns the whole thing very rapidly into a demonic temptation to experiment in homosexual activity to "see" if is true. There is a compulsive nature to the whole thing, as we've seen in Matthew's and Stan's story.

Homosexuality Related to Traumatic Experiences in Childhood

Ruell's and Loren's Stories

Homosexual rape, leaving in its wake unresolved and unhealed trauma, a badly wounded self-image, and a monstrous sense of guilt (from participation in the act, albeit unwilling), can later open the victim to fears that he is homosexual, and from there it can lead into overt homosexuality. These incidences often happen to boys who are "psychologically" unprotected in one way or another. Ruell's case illustrates what I mean by this.

His father deserted him when he was an infant, and his mother and grandmother raised him. Any visitors who happened in were usually of the feminine gender and were friends of his mother, grandmother, and an aunt or two who had at different times boarded in the home. There were almost no men, much less strong or whole men, for him to love and pattern after. This situation alone had the effect of stunting his masculine development. Hungry for masculine friendship, he timidly struck up an acquaintance with an older man, and this suddenly culminated in a shocking and humiliating homosexual rape. Shamed and horrified, he could never tell anybody what had happened.

Later on, failing to achieve a secure sexual identity after puberty, he began to fear that he was himself homosexual. This fear very seriously scarred and shaped his life for a good number of years before he found the healing he so direly needed. Had his father been a warm and present reality in his life, his grievous reaction to the homosexual rape would likely have been resolved and healed, or at least modified in a different direction. In fact, for several reasons the thing probably would not have happened at all. A protecting father is a strong deterrent to such offenders.

When our lack of spiritual knowledge allows it, Satan can take occasion by the sins of others against us to work in us the same sickness. The fears and temptations that follow such an occurrence are his work. Such a memory, unhealed, plays havoc with the imaginative life; through it, an unwanted door is opened into the mind. Through it, lust attempts to enter. One is then embroiled in spiritual warfare.

The shock of exposure to pornographic materials or to group orgies in masturbation can affect a young mind in much the same way as homosexual rape. Such an exposure *is* a rape of the mind that opens the door for the homosexual compulsions that can come later. This shock is compounded when adult men are the instruments through which the exposure comes.

The primary need, of course, is for healing of the traumatic memory itself. In this prayer, the victim forgives the one who has so monstrously sinned against him. The effects of this sin are bound together and cast away from him in such a way that he is no longer either shaped or pained by them. Then, in whatever way the Holy Spirit leads, our Lord is invited into the memory and healing and cleansing take place. False guilt, as well as any real guilt that came later, is dealt with and removed. Sometimes there is a grudge against God, and this too is confessed. The memory of the event is not obliterated, but the pain is removed. One can think of it without the old shame and humiliation. In such a case, after praying for release from any demonic oppression (i.e., casting out any oppressing spirit of sexual lust), I pray for the *closing* of that door into the mind through which has entered such a sear on the imagination, such fear, confusion, and humiliation to the heart.

Ruell's case is one of the more obvious ones in this category. Cases that are much less obvious, but are all too common, concern infantile experiences of rejection due to gender or even birth deformity.

Loren, a trim, good-looking man in his early forties, had been overtly homosexual from his adolescent years. This had caused severe conflicts between himself and his father, and a rift with the rest of the family. He disapproved of himself, yet vigorously defended his behavior in arguments with his dad. He realized that within his homosexuality were elements of resentment and rebellion toward his father, but he had never known how to handle them. This man had come to Christ and been genuinely converted, but he struggled without a lasting victory against his lifelong homosexual orientation until God brought to awareness the root memory. This happened as we asked the Lord to find and enter into the memory that would reveal the genesis of his problem.[7] This prayer led immediately into his reliving a scene that occurred within minutes after his birth.

As the scene unfolded, he saw his father walk into the bedroom where he had just been delivered. Disappointment suddenly filled the room and weighed heavily upon him. His father looked at him in what he described as disgust and said, "Another boy!" With this, his father turned and wheeled out of the room, for he was the third son and a daughter had been greatly desired. All this Loren "saw" and lived through again—this time comprehending it conceptually as well as with the heart. This rejection explained why Loren had later on, much to the consternation of the family, tried to become the girl in the family. He wanted to play with dolls, and with girls instead of boys. Unconsciously, he tried to be the girl his father had wanted.

Ruell and Loren found the healing they had so long sought, healings that brought joyful releases into freedom. Both are now fully in touch with their masculine identities and both are happily married.

Birth Trauma and Repression of Masculinity

Christ can enter into and heal prenatal, birth, and early infantile trauma without the necessity of the person reliving the memory. In cases of known infant trauma, the parents can lay hands on their little one and pray, knowing that our Lord will walk into those memories of pain and heal their infant, banishing fear from it, enabling it to receive their love. After this initial prayer, the father and mother can continue from time to time with prayer and laying on of hands as the infant sleeps, asking the Lord to enter into the little one more and more, shedding abroad His love and light into the deep heart of the infant.

The mother can pray specifically that He enable her infant to receive her love, and with it a healthy sense of its unique being. As she prays, and by way of releasing her faith, she can draw joyful faith-pictures in her mind of this happening and, lifting them up into God's light for His blessing, she can give thanks that it is even now being done. The father can, of course, pray in the same manner, and be confident that as the head of his family, there is a special protection that comes to his entire family through him and his prayers. Other examples of healings taking place apart from bringing up the memories would include instances when adults have experienced a deep peace and a removal of emotional blocks after prayer for healing of infantile trauma.

Sometimes, however, the person relives the full experience. When this happens, we see quite vividly how the physical and psychological pain can be of such an intensity that the hurting "infant" within the full-grown person is still fearful of being outside the womb, a condition that represses the true self, and with it, true masculinity.[8]

One such healing was of a young husband and father who was absolutely unable to drive his car in open country outside the city or ever board an airplane. He could not understand why he had to exercise courage to make the first move out of bed in the morning, and then again to leave his home for work. He had been treated for these phobias and fears, but they seemed to get worse rather than better. He and his wife were weary of trying to deal with his problems, and were concerned that his ability to earn a living would be further restricted.

I had no idea what his problem was, but we had no sooner gone to prayer for him than he was into his birth experience, a very traumatic one indeed. I knew nothing of this before we went to prayer, and didn't need to, for soon I "saw" and relived with him the whole painful drama of his birth experience. As we were praying, he began to see (not knowing what it was) a small circle of light. Momentarily he informed me, "I am being born," and instantly we both knew the light he was seeing was at the end of the birth canal. All had been normal in the birth to that point.

Then began the torturous contortions of a difficult birth. His shoulders worked desperately to push his head through to the light. Then he was choking, face down, the cord around his neck, while at the same time his chest was being crushed; the pain was excruciating. I was seeing each terrible moment and ministering to him in it as if the birth were actually occurring. I prayed for God's mercy and help for him as he came through the birth channel, for relief and release as he choked on the cord, and for healing and cessation of the pain in his chest. The memory of the pain in his chest was the most excruciating of all, and had remained in his unconscious memories as a dreadful thing indeed.

Then I prayed for the unspeakable aloneness he felt after he was laid aside, untended, cold, yet in severe pain, while his mother was being attended to. The doctor's face loomed up as something to be dreadfully feared. (It is important to note that he had an almost pathological fear of this physician in later years, though he did not know why. Also, in moments of stress he would unaccountably choke, just as he had done in reliving the memory of the cord around his neck.)

As the reliving of the painful birth ended, I asked the Lord to wrap the little one in the blanket of His love, and this the man experienced as the healing of all those memories began. He cried, making the sounds of a newborn infant. That he *could* make such sounds astonished me.

This man was one who until healed of birth trauma was still afraid to be outside the womb. Hence his fear of open spaces. With this healing he gradually attained normalcy. It is easy to see how one's masculinity would be terribly suppressed by the fears[9] and phobias such a birth experience could leave in a life. He had seriously doubted his masculinity, and had never been able to think well of himself as a man among men.

There are birth injuries that so traumatize an infant that it is rendered unable to receive its mother's love—a position of being schizoid in relation to her. This man was one of the more fortunate ones because he had not receded back into the womb, psychologically speaking, to the extent that he could not receive his mother's love and with it a sense of *being*. Even though he had suffered several breakdowns and undergone psychiatric treatment for the greater part of his life, he was less injured than he might have been. He was simply fearful to be outside the womb, and had a very great need for healing of the infantile memories of physical pain.

Johnny's Story

Johnny was married and in his mid-twenties when his father died. It was then that he, a very needy person, moved into homosexuality, a sexual behavior he practiced for two years.

His deep inner craving still unmet and his marriage in serious trouble, Johnny attempted to extricate himself from his homosexual activity. It was then that he found Christ and, thoroughly converted, became an ardent witness to the faith.

About ten years after his conversion, however, and all of them spent as a devout and wholly committed Christian, Johnny began falling apart. He feared his children would find out what he had been, he feared his wife would leave him, but most of all he had a dreadful fear of failure. In addition to these fears, his homosexual compulsions were once again too strong for his conscious mind to deny or repress, and he feared he was, in truth, deviant. He was in the midst of a nervous breakdown.

It was in this state of collapse that he responded to his wife's concerned urging and came for prayer. His conscious mind, so wearied with repressing all the old fears, denials, and bad memories, had ceased to do its job. Johnny would now have to face his inner loneliness, all the fears and darkness he had so long refused to see and acknowledge.

His story is a terrible one. It has to do with a brutalizing father, and with older brothers who practiced homosexuality as part of the pecking-order syndrome at work in the home.

His father had never had a smile or kind word for him, something he had yearned for all his life. As his sisters grew up, he had to live with the fact that his father was molesting them sexually, and that he could do nothing about it. He also watched his father choose girlfriends for his older sons, and then seduce them himself. These sons, brutalized by their father, spent time in prison, and became involved in the brute kind of homosexuality that prisons are rife with. They would then come home and abuse the younger boys in a similar fashion. Johnny, the youngest, seemed to catch the worst brunt of their dehumanizing behavior.

No wonder Johnny was breaking apart. All these memories were festering within, as yet unhealed. His masculinity had, of course, been seriously repressed in the environment he had grown up in.

After he had shared his story with me, one that he had never been able fully to tell before, we went to prayer. Although he knew that prayer was the only way, he at first resisted. This was because he thought prayer was more or less an exercise of the conscious mind, and that he would have to try to understand and deal with the whole problem consciously again. And that was precisely what he could no longer do, what he was worn out from attempting to do. That was when I asked him to relax completely and let me do the praying, while he simply looked up to Jesus with the eyes of his heart. His healing illustrates the inestimable value of "picturing" or imagining. Besides being a valid way of "seeing," it opens the heart to any pictures God would send. God sends us His help and truth, and often it comes as a "picture." Johnny's healing also illustrates how closely hate can be connected to love.

Realizing there was hatred toward his father, I asked him to picture his father standing next to Jesus. It is very difficult to look up and see Jesus when one's heart is filled with hate. And it is also difficult to picture the face of the one we hate. We tend to blot it out, annihilate it. Johnny couldn't look up to picture Jesus or his father, but yielding to the Presence of the Lord and with his head bent down almost to the floor, he began to sob uncontrollably as the deep-seated hatred toward his father welled up and out of his heart. He then had to forgive his father, and this forgiveness had to come from the deepest recesses of Johnny's wounded heart. It seemed to him an absolute impossibility. Even so, he knew he had to get through this impasse, for he could not go on in the old tormented way. I assured him that loving and forgiving another is a matter of the *will* rather than the emotions, and that his feelings naturally reflected the abuses of his early years with his father.

Praying that his *will* be strengthened, and insisting that he picture his father, I asked him to *will* to stretch up his hand and take the hand of his father. His head still bent, he slowly lifted his arm up as if to take the hand of his father, sobbing, "I *will* to forgive you, Dad. I *will* to forgive you." I asked him to look up into his father's face and say, "Father, I *do* forgive you." Then, to my astonishment, torrents of repressed love began to pour out. Johnny cried over and over and over, "Daddy, I love you, Daddy, I love you. I *do* forgive you. Jesus, forgive me for hating him. Jesus, forgive me. Jesus, help me." And then, to his dad, "If only you could have said one kind word to me." At this, he slowly looked up to see the face that in life had always appeared so stern and hostile to him. I shall never forget his amazement as he "saw" his dad's face. "My father is *smiling* at me! He is smiling at me!" he exclaimed.

I do not fully understand the smile that seemed to assuage a lifetime of yearning on Johnny's part, but I've seen this sort of thing happen far too often, along with the lasting wholesome fruit it bears, to ever doubt it. Can it be that there is something about forgiving that releases not only the living, but the dead as well? Can the dead know when they are released from another's unforgiveness? This is wonderful to speculate on, and of course we can only speculate. But this I know—when we heal in Jesus' name, He sends us healing pictures as well as healing words. Jesus was in charge of that smile. This also I know—in Johnny's prayer of forgiveness, he came into a relationship with his father, one that he had never been able to achieve in his dad's lifetime.

You will remember that Johnny began to search out homosexual partners only after his father's death. In his heart, he had always yearned to win his father's love and affirmation—that one smile. His dad's death, before any of this happened, left the injured little boy in Johnny crying out for that father-love, crying out for the masculine identity that could come with it. Perhaps he was in part looking for his father in these relationships. He was certainly, like Matthew, searching for himself in another. He was in the grip of an acute identity crisis.

In forgiving his father, Johnny set the stage for his release from fear of failure. This fear was no mere weed in the garden of his heart, but a massive choking root that was threatening his entire inner life, and that is how it appeared in the picture that came as I prayed. Prayer for its removal seemed like prayer for the pulling up of an ugly old tree, roots and all. I prayed that the roots be loosened by God's love and power flowing in; and as this began to happen, I saw the fear come up and out of Johnny. I then asked for Jesus to fill with His freeing, healing love all the spaces where the awful root tentacles had been. We waited as we saw this happening, and until there was no fear left in his heart.

Like the lame man who when healed went into the Temple leaping and praising God,[10] Johnny's reaction to finding himself set free was ecstatic. Having long sought the Lord and this healing, he was overwhelmed in its reality. His joy was a blessed thing to see.

In Johnny, we see the unhealed trauma of homosexual rape in childhood, the utter repression of masculinity by a hostile father and environment, and the terrible yearning for a father's love and his own identity all mixed in one. His major healing came as he was released from the repressed hatred toward his father and was enabled to forgive him.

Inordinate Self-love: Or Is It Inordinate Insecurity?

Randy's Story

Randy, an exceedingly creative young man, had been successful in intellectual and artistic pursuits far beyond his peers, and sometimes his tutors as well. I first met him when he began to realize that he could not share his life with others, including girls. He simply had no time for them. They interfered with his art.

A real live woman is a lot of trouble. Charles Williams's masterpiece, *Descent into Hell*, shockingly images one man's fall when he elects to love himself in exclusion to the more troublesome and time-consuming flesh-and-blood woman. In her place he takes to himself a succubus, an occult term for an imaginary woman. This is, in actuality, the practice of masturbation with an accompanying fantasy life. The reader watches him deteriorate as his grasp on a real woman loosens, and the illusory world he step by step *chooses* becomes at once more important, compulsive, and even horrifyingly bleak to him. We then see his deliberate and devastating descent into the hell of the false or narcissistic self.

Randy, with his valid need for time and solitude in which to pursue his art, was having trouble learning how to carry in his one person the artistic gifts God had endowed him with. Before learning, he was in danger of going the way of Wentworth, the character in Williams's novel. Young, inexperienced in many respects, and still stuck in the narcissistic phase of his existence, he was for awhile not too uncomfortable there, because his gifts had won a place for him among his fellows. He had moved, as he now realized, with a good deal of smug self-satisfaction in the security this afforded. Unlike Wentworth, however, he began to see his false pride and wanted to be rid of it. He began to discover and face up to a certain disdain within himself toward others, not unusual—but prideful and wrong just the same—for one who oftener than not finds himself among the more plodding types.

He also found himself in bondage to the habit of masturbation, a thing that had long been with him. He had tried to convince himself that it was after all harmless enough. The articles he had read on the subject stated there was really nothing wrong with it. Now, however, the matter and habit of masturbation had become an obsession, one that was never far from his mind. It was a blow to his pride to admit that the habit had him, rather than the other way around, and that furthermore *the accompanying temptations and fantasies were turning into homosexual ones*.

Along with these developments, which were seriously shaking his ideal image of himself, came the hardest blow yet to his pride. His most respected mentors were saying there was something wrong with his ability to fully express his artistic talent. Gifted in several areas of the arts, he was functioning below his ability in each, and his tutors were frank in facing him with this disconcerting fact. In criticizing his differing works, his mentors would point to one moderate success after another and say, "Look, this is good, but it is not nearly what you have within you to give. What is wrong? Why can't you give it out?"

Randy's problem with masturbation, a form of the wrong kind of self-love continued past puberty, was beginning to take its toll in several ways. His temptation to homosexuality, another form of inordinate self-love and one he was beginning to dally with and attempt to act out, *was simply an extension of the practice of masturbation*. The same need lurks behind both forms of narcissistic love.

In prayer for some whose homosexuality falls into this grouping, all too often the root memory that comes up will be one of masturbating, either alone or in a group. These will not simply be occasions of childish curiosity or of false guilt incurred, but will mark a time when the lust came in and took root. When the sin involved in this memory is confessed, healing can come quickly, for we have gotten at the genesis of the thing. With the root, the whole unhealthy plant of inordinate self-love can be pulled up. To pull this up is one very important thing; to heal by allowing God's love to pour into and penetrate the rents and empty holes left by such a weed is another. The minister is always to pray in such a way that the heart receives this healing inflow of God's love and Spirit. Again at this point I would reiterate that I have never yet prayed for a man with homosexual problems (in any grouping) who did not also have problems with masturbation. Both are harmful to personality development when persisted in and, as Randy came to realize, to artistic development as well. As we shall see later, however, there was more behind Randy's problem than merely lust.

Randy needed a powerful exhortation and a prayerful push in the direction of *a dying*. But death to the wrong kind of self-love (a practice of the presence of the old man) was a choice he and he alone could make. My work as a minister, besides calling him in no uncertain terms to this death, was to paint as best I could the picture of what his vibrant true self would be. It was to invoke the Presence of Jesus in such a way that Randy could look up to Him and hear Him say, "What does a man gain by winning the whole world at the cost of his true self?" It was unswervingly to point Randy to Jesus in order that he might be drawn up and out of the hell of separation and into a full union with God and the realization of his new self.

This is a call to a heroic existence, one that demands a full conversion of the *will*. Therefore, besides confession and turning from the specific sin of inordinate love of self—and the sins of pride, masturbation, homosexuality that went along with it—Randy had to choose to make his *will* one with Christ's, and to come alive in absolute commitment to Him as Lord. To help him do this, I gave him the assignment of going through the Gospels, and personalizing every word of Christ to His people. He was to write these out in his prayer journal as if Christ were addressing him solely. For example, Matthew 22:37 would read as follows: "Randy, you are to love the Lord your God with all your heart and with all your soul and with all your mind." Randy was then to listen to God in order to carry out this, the greatest commandment. In this way, he would come to know Jesus as Lord.

Randy went away and began to practice this obedience, and with obedience he began to get understanding. This obedience is so radical that it sometimes takes months before the full import of that to which the disciple is called fully sinks in. So it was with Randy. But through this obedience he slowly began to get in touch with his own inner being and make all that was in his heart and mind present to God. All of him was thus brought into conversation with God: his past, his present, his thought life, and his imaginative life. In this way he got in touch with and understood his problems as an artist. Soon a letter came, and the following excerpts and illustrations from it reveal his new understanding of the effects of masturbation upon his personal and creative life:

"The word [masturbation]," he writes, "has been on my mind . . . along with a picture."

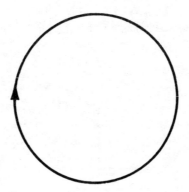

"Masturbation, physically, is a self-bent thing. Its focus is inward. It doesn't share. It doesn't know the verb 'to give.' It is a fire that feeds itself. Hence the picture. Life encircled by a ring of guilt."

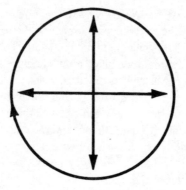

"A shell that inhibits freedom. . . . A tremendous self-repulsion ensues. A physical loneliness. A lack of self-acceptance."

These descriptions of what his personal life had been were in truth parallel to his problems as an artist. He was unable to freely and fully give out to others from his rich store of artistic talent. Therefore he says:

"The diagram needs badly to be like this":

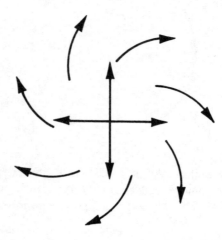

"Loosened! Open! Sharing! Free! The richness [of his creative ideas in writing, painting, acting] is now allowed to flow freely from within to out. Not just seething around inside. Not hoarding self. But sharing generously."

About his self-regarding habit that had inhibited his artistic life, he says: "We are talking about years of deeply entrenched pain and practice. Years of deluding self-satisfaction." His letter ends with a cry to God, "Father, come and crack this shell!"

Randy has expressed in his letter the same understanding of the effects of this habit on the imaginative and personal life as C. S. Lewis did in answering a query about the nature of the habit of masturbation and its effects on those who come "to love the prison."

For me the real evil of masturbation would be that it takes an appetite which, in lawful use, leads the individual out of himself to complete (and correct) his own personality in that of another (and finally in children and even grandchildren) and turns it back; sends the man back into the prison of himself, there to keep a harem of imaginary brides. And this harem, once admitted, works against his *ever* getting out and really uniting with a real woman. For the harem is always accessible, always subservient, calls for no sacrifices or adjustments, and can be endowed with erotic and psychological attractions which no real woman can rival. Among those shadowy brides he is always adored, always the perfect lover; no demand is made on his unselfishness, no mortification ever imposed on his vanity. In the end, they become merely the medium through which he increasingly adores himself. Do read Charles Williams' *Descent into Hell* and study the character of Mr. Wentworth. And it is not only the faculty of love which is thus sterilized, forced back on itself, but also the faculty of the imagination. The true exercise of imagination in my view, is (a) To help us to understand other people, (b) To respond to, and, some of us, to produce art. But it has also a bad use: to provide for us, in shadowy form, a substitute for virtues, successes, distinctions, etc. which ought to be sought *outside* in the real world—e.g., picturing all I'd do if I were rich instead of earning and saving. Masturbation involves this abuse of imagination in erotic matters (which I think bad in itself) and thereby encourages a similar abuse of it in all spheres. After all, almost the *main* work of life is to *come out* of our selves, out of the little, dark prison we are all born in. Masturbation is to be avoided as *all* things are to be avoided which retard this process. The danger is that of coming to *love* the prison.[11]

A descent into the hell of self (inordinate self-love)—whether by attachment to a particular sin, by a trek through the occult, by sloth and passivity, or however—is harmful to the creative imagination.

Because heaven and earth are crammed with living creatures and concrete things, awesome to know in their realness, man is only becoming whole while reaching out to them, i.e., when he is outer-directed. He can only know himself by knowing others, by coming to taste, in a manner of speaking, the incredible variety of *isness* that resides outside himself. Solomon expresses this in part by his proverb: "Iron sharpens iron, and one man sharpens another."[12]

It is in loving God, other men, and all creatures for themselves that we begin to partake of their goodness and beauty. Looking at and loving that which is other than ourselves, we begin to "incarnate" it. This is vital to artistic growth, just as it is to spiritual and psychological growth. Alienation in the form of introspection, self-love, enclosure in the circle or sphere of subjectivity is not the way to know oneself; outer-directed interaction with the objectively real is. To know and love God is the beginning of all joy, and it can yield the gift of a divine self-forgetfulness which is the secret of great art.

Ruth Tiffany Barnhouse rightly attacks the popular notion that homosexuality and creativity are linked. She exposes the inexcusable lack of scholarly accuracy in articles and books we are bombarded with in regard to this:

Homosexual apologists . . . have continued the practice of drawing personal biographical inferences from works of art in an apparent attempt to arrogate to themselves a substantial portion, if not the lion's share, of the world's creativity. There is no evidence whatsoever to support such claims. In fact, contemporary psychological research shows that on tests designed to measure creativity and divergent thinking, heterosexuals tend to perform better than homosexuals.[13]

She goes on to warn that

the notion that creativity and male homosexuality are linked remains in the public imagination, and in some instances may even have the force of a self-fulfilling prophecy. A boy with artistic talent who is told often enough that this is a sign of homosexual tendencies may believe it and eventually act on it, especially if the rest of his upbringing is equally benighted.[14]

But there is, I believe, a reason (apart from the inaccurate scholarship on the subject) that this idea has remained so strongly rooted in the public imagination. From the experience I've had in seeing sexual neuroses healed, I believe that artistic people are particularly plagued with temptations to homosexuality and other forms of sexual promiscuity, and there is a reason why this should be so. As I wrote in *Real Presence,*

when the intuitive faculty is developed apart from the work of the Holy Spirit, and/or apart from the good of reason, sexuality so often becomes in both art and religion, a *numinosum.* Sexual idolatry of one kind or another then ensues. Whether in art or in religion, the dark force often first fastens on man's procreative functions (whether by fantasy or act) and by this brings him into bondage. The force that can never create but can only destroy would start the process of death in a man at that very point where God intended man to give life.[15]

I have seen these temptations to be, time after time, a demonic attempt to bereave of artistic talent—to cut it short, truncate it. The artist's intuitive faculty is the receptor for the

Real—that is, for the true. He cannot be servant both to the Real and to its delusory imitation or substitute. The artist's duty, as Aleksandr Solzhenitsyn has reminded us, is to be a receptor for that "one word of truth that outweighs the world."[16] This *word* enables the artist (even as it did Solzhenitsyn himself) to rise above the mind-set and the prejudices of the age and thereby, through his art, to deliver others from it. The great artist reveals truth, justice, and beauty to a world blinded by lies, injustice, and the despairingly bleak. This one word of truth, holding as it does both justice and beauty, is not apprehended by the mind that has continually opened itself to delusive fantasies. These fantasies usher in not only the images of inordinate sexual gratification, but a lying word (delusion) that in the end fragments the person and his world.

As we stated earlier, Randy had been stuck in the narcissistic phase, that wrong kind of self-love. Once he faced that selfishness and pride which is the lot of every human being, Randy was able to see his inner story. His soul could then begin to acknowledge its very great need of affirmation, its terrible lifelong fear of failure. He could begin to read the true tale of his life. The flipside of the wrong kind of self-love will always be some form of self-hatred. Inordinate self-love which is, psychologically speaking, an immaturity in the personality, is the reverse face of a deep insecurity.

Randy saw that his inability to share his life with others (his egocentric selfishness if you please—for this is the spiritual dimension of the problem, and also what it appeared both to himself and others to be) was psychologically "an enormous lack—trying so hard to be covered . . . a relentless overcompensation in order to survive with the self. . . ." It was an inordinate *insecurity*. About the old habit of masturbation, he writes:

> Now I see the compulsive masturbation that infected me even clearer in light of that question that I perpetually faced as a young boy—Would I turn out all right? That tremendous

unsurety left deep feelings of insecurity and fear of finally being rejected. This is why the illusion of being King was so fully and frantically adopted. I had to appear in deep love with myself to be sure to coax others to like me too. Unfortunately it drove them away before it attracted them. The masturbation has got to be seen as that which was adopted to make things seem all right. . . . I clearly see now that that's all masturbation ever was—a desperate need to feel okay. . . . I don't know if I believe that a case of compulsive masturbation can begin without deep dread and anxiety every time. . . . The need almost leaves the area of sex altogether in that it has more to do with trying to make a way for the psyche to survive. . . . I believe it is *no* survival at all, but a siren's song leading the frightened soul into a prison of lies which lead to still deeper and more binding inner cells of destruction and despair.

Long before this letter arrived, God had answered his prayer and "cracked the shell," bringing him into a position of unusual strength and maturity, one enriched by his imaginative and intellectual giftedness. His maturity was quickly tested by the fire of adversity and personal sorrow; yet he grew in understanding, strength, and in genuine love and humility. In reference to the adversity, he writes:

Somehow by seeing this, I have been even further strengthened these most difficult days when affirmation around my daily walk is scarce. By the clear seeing I can choose freely not to stoop to the cheap trick—the rubber crutch of masturbation. I can see that when the drive comes, it has much more to do with needing to feel okay. The prayer is then *not* "Lord, stop my sexual drive." No!—that is normal and healthy—but rather, "Lord, I claim the very large YES that You have said and are saying and will always say for me." *There* is the only source of finding affirmation. . . .

I can strongly say that He has freed me. He has broken the bonds of that closed and dying circle. More and more the creative forces within me are reaching out. . . . It has taken time to learn how to give.

Only one who knows the story he is now living out can know how thoroughly and wonderfully Randy has learned to give. And in that giving, the real Randolph has emerged—gifts and all.

The Animal Self

The sins of the flesh are bad, but they are the least bad of all sins. All the worst pleasures are purely spiritual: the pleasure of putting other people in the wrong, of bossing and patronising and spoiling sport, and backbiting; the pleasures of power, of hatred. For there are two things inside me, competing with the human self which I must try to become. They are the Animal self, and the Diabolical self. The Diabolical self is the worse of the two. That is why a cold, self-righteous prig who goes regularly to church may be far nearer to hell than a prostitute. But, of course, it is better to be neither.[17]

The relation of the natural to the spiritual is one of continuous conversion. . . . Our natural life must not rule, God must rule in us.[18]

Having considered inordinate self-love in Randy's case, one that had the psychological flipside of inordinate insecurity, we need to look for a moment at two other headings under which homosexual behavior can fall, those of *concupiscence* and *rebellion*. Concupiscence and rebellion are elements finally to be found in all homosexual behavior, but in certain cases these appear as chief conditions to be dealt with and healed. In one the animal self dominates; in the other the diabolical rules in concert with the animal self. The true tale of these lives will be found to have its psychological flipside as well, an unmet basic need in the personality which can be healed through prayer.

We have seen in fiction and in real life persons who are like Johnny's father: brutal themselves and instrumental in others becoming so. Such a one is ruled to a horrifying degree by the physical and spiritual lusts of body and soul. Somewhere along the line, for whatever reason, the animal and the diabolical selves gained their tyrannical ascendancy.

Adolescents, with easy access to drugs and alcohol, can quickly close themselves off from the higher and more reasoned responses to life, not to mention the spiritually sensitive ones. Through the resulting apathy and failure to choose the good (an act of the *will*), they not only fail to mature in their personal and sexual identities, but the animal self can easily become the dominant one. As an unchecked tyrant, aided and abetted by the permissive and sensate culture in which we live, it can grow increasingly violent and perverted in its sexual appetites and quite effectively put to death the emerging human self. In some cases, therefore, we find the chief problem to have been one of passively and progressively allowing the animal self to dominate. The writer of Ecclesiasticus speaks (in 23:16) of the destruction to both body and soul such an uncontrolled inner tyrant wields:

> Hot lust that blazes like a fire can never be quenched till life is destroyed. A man whose whole body is given to sensuality never stops till the fire consumes him.

Inherent in the healing of every Christian is the ongoing deliverance from inordinate love of the self. This, the affliction of all, *is* the Fall in every life. It is pride. What I am writing about here is apropos to the story of every life. We can all understand it because we have all to one extent or another experienced it. And we know too, if we are given to reflection on the matter, that in any descent into the hell of self-love the animal (as well as the diabolical) self begins to dominate.

If we have learned the joy of discipline, and the freeing authority this brings to the true self, we well know how this came about. We know how we ourselves were healed, and therefore we have the same prescription for those caught in even the most perverted and bestial of practices. I've said this for the sake of all who pray with others for healing, because I know how easy it is to run from certain needs in the lives of people.

I still remember the first person who came for help and confessed certain sexual practices with a beast. In fear and trembling the person was finally able to choke out the confession. Had I shown the least shock or fear of the terrible compulsion gripping this person, one that was wrecking his life, he would have been lost. I simply moved quickly against the darkness killing the person, and saw the real self go free. To speak of compulsions is also to speak of that part of the personality ruled, or in danger of being ruled, by something other than God. Christ came in to free what had been, in this case, a very bleak and empty "house of the soul," and to fill it with His glory. The human self, uniting with its Lord, then began to take the proper authority over soul and body, putting to death (Colossians 3:5) every defiling lust. The total person (spirit, soul, and body) was freed not only to live fully, but to realize its incredible privilege of *becoming.* Now, years later when on the rare occasions in my travels I see this person, I still marvel at the beauty and the power to witness that fills this precious life.

The Diabolical Self

In his book, *I Prayed, He Answered,* Pastor William Vaswig tells of his son Phillip's dynamic healing. Diagnosed incurably schizophrenic, he was healed when Agnes Sanford prayed with him. Phillip, now in a responsible ministry to others, repeatedly states that *rebellion* of the deepest kind was at the bottom of his illness. Any and every dread thing can issue from a state of unrighteous rebellion, and there are times when it is chief among the causes spawning homosexual and lesbian behavior.

For example, there are instances where lesbian behavior is connected to fear and hatred of the father or of some other man. Hatred toward one man generalizes to others and the woman then begins for various reasons, among them vengeance, to sexualize her relationships with other women. A seed of hate, growing up, gives rise to a wilderness of hatred and rebellion. And rebellion, as the prophet Samuel tells us, "is as the sin of witchcraft."[19] Out of it, any and every kind of perversion can come. "Vengeance is mine; I will repay, saith the Lord,"[20] but the diabolical self wants vengeance. Here we see the collaboration of the animal and the diabolical selves. Of the two, as C.S. Lewis has said, the diabolical is the worse.

I have noted on a number of occasions how hard it is for a young person to curb the animal and the diabolical selves when their parents have failed to do it for them as children. The young child cannot at first curb them for himself. He learns self-discipline by having been wisely disciplined. Fortunate is the child who, when in the throes of a tantrum, sloth, or some other harmful disorder, has parents who are loving and wise enough to take the proper authority over these baser passions.

So the child learns to curb the animal and the diabolical selves as he learns to *will* that which is right and good.

When the animal or the diabolical self has long ruled a life, I call the *will* of that person to the fore, helping him or her to get in touch with this faculty of their personality. And I pray specifically for the healing of a will that has never developed or has atrophied through disuse. I call these persons to choices: "Choose ye this day whom ye will serve." "Choose Heaven or Hell, *now*. If you want to continue in the way you have, we won't waste time praying. But if you choose Heaven, I'll help you onto the path." "Choose now to know who you *really* are, and we will see you set free this day and on the road to becoming all God created you to be." In these and many other ways, rather than arguing or dialoguing with the animal or diabolical self I call the apathetic will to a choice. This is not only to keep from wasting time (which is reason enough), but is also to challenge the will that has far too long passively practiced the presence of the old man. And I am not called to help anyone practice *that* presence. I am called to help all I can into the Presence of a holy God, One who calls us to richly partake of His holiness.

Lesbian Relationships

Bette's and Bonita's Stories

Bette, a native of New England, loved to explore the mountainous regions of the Northeast. This afforded some comfort for the inner dissatisfaction that seemed always to be part of even her finest moments. She had been married for several years, not altogether happily, and had enjoyed good success in her profession, but that too had failed to satisfy a yearning she had inside. She felt a chasm or gap inside herself. Something needed filling in; a gap needed bridging. She thought she needed more love than her husband, a man not given to warm and thoughtful responses, could give. She had all her life been drawn toward women for the affection she craved, and had finally become involved in a lesbian relationship with her best friend. She knew it was wrong and was plagued with guilt over it. Too, she was fearful that her husband or others in the community whom she served so well would find out about it. She had left off the relationship several times, only to return to it, and now felt unable to extricate herself from it without help. She had turned to Christ and desired with all her heart the help He could give her.

Her present problem, so completely beyond her understanding, quickly became apparent to me as I asked about her childhood. As an infant and throughout her childhood, her father had forbidden her mother to pick her up and hold her. He had been influenced by the Harvard psychologist, B. F. Skinner, who raised his daughter in a box. But his main idea differed from Skinner's in that he was merely determined to keep his daughter "unspoiled."

As a result of his thinking, Bette's mother, basically a warm and loving person, suffered terribly (since such treatment went against nature). But she suffered silently and remained in full compliance with her husband's wishes. As a result of this, the chief pain of Bette's childhood was the frustrated desire to nestle in her mother's arms. When we prayed, the memory that came to the surface, brimful of sorrow, was of herself as a tiny girl, desperately wanting to be hugged tightly to her mother's breast. When this didn't happen, she had thrown her arms around the washing machine instead, and hugged it to herself.

Another example is that of Bonita, a recent convert to Christ, and one quite active in helping others find Him. A busy wife and mother, her fall came after an intelligent, sophisticated woman joined their sharing and Bible study group and continued to come while maintaining a position of unbelief. This woman was a psychiatrist, and in attempting to convert her, Bonita instead found herself being comforted in moments of stress by the doctor. In a critical moment of extreme weariness and distress, the woman's embraces went too far, and Bonita soon found herself locked in a lesbian relationship with one who was experienced in this behavior. In great anguish of heart she asked, "How could this possibly have happened to me?" She boarded a plane and traveled many miles to find the answer to this question, as well as the help she needed to extricate herself from the other woman's skillful clutches.

As in Bette's case, she too had experienced the dreadful deprivation of a mother's arms. Though she had become a joyful and enthusiastic Christian, the memories of early rejections still ached within her, still helped to shape her existence. Her history included the fact that her mother had unsuccessfully tried to abort her even though a previous pregnancy had been successfully terminated, facts the mother did not hesitate to tell Bonita when she was yet a small child. Her mother, defeated in the attempt to destroy her as an unborn child, had always openly resented her for intruding into her life, and actively hated her for any affection she received from her father. The pain of these circumstances had always been with Bonita. In the unguarded moment when the woman she was seeking to win to Christ very comfortingly held her, even as a mother would a crying child, Bonita simply melted into her arms. Then when the doctor continued her "treatment," Bonita did not have the will to resist.

I have added these two histories, briefly recounted, to emphasize what has already been shown in Lisa's story related earlier. The fact is that so very often the one who falls into a lesbian relationship does so as Lisa, Bette, and Bonita did—in an unguarded moment, and out of a severe deprivation of a mother's loving arms in infancy and childhood. Bette's and Bonita's healing, like Lisa's, came as they allowed Christ to come into the midst of their inner loneliness, and heal the old deprivations and rejections. In forgiving their mothers and all other persons involved, in releasing any bitterness they felt over the early circumstances of their lives, and in confessing and turning from their sins, each received God's love and healing into the gnawingly empty spaces where once only the hollow, aching memories of a missing mother-love knocked about.

Cases Where Infantile Deprivation Is Not the Prime Factor

I have seen cases where lesbian behavior is connected to a woman's need to be set free from the effects of having an extremely possessive and dominating mother. Two were so identical that I tell them as one in order to stress this particular need for healing of the soul. These two attractive married women, their stories strikingly similar yet entirely unrelated, realized (alarmingly enough) that their lesbian behavior would not have occurred before their entrance into the Church. I will speak of what they had in common in order to show why this could be.

Both women entered into the world of loving and satisfying relationships only after they were converted to Christ and began to be part of a body of caring Christians. This was tremendously exciting for them, and each in her own respective geographical sphere had great freedom to share her newfound joy with others. Also, both were strong women, and once freed to relate meaningfully to others, their leadership capacities came to the fore. Each, however, fell into a lesbian relationship after failing to realize that her understanding of what it means to love another was faulty. Moreover, neither could discern the difference between *agape*, God's love that heals, and the human loves—affection, friendship, and *eros*, erotic love—through which they were attempting to minister. At the very least, the kinds of love got grievously mixed in their attempts to help a close friend, and each woman ended by misusing and perverting the human loves in order to meet her own needs and the needs of another.

Behind this behavior was a possessive and dominating mother, one they'd fled from geographically, but were still tied to emotionally and psychologically. This was evident in their attempts to appease and please their mothers, though both knew this to be an impossible task. Their very telephones were threatening instruments, the wires of which could at any moment turn into grotesque umbilical cords connecting them again to mom's voice and mom's will. Yet *each still craved her mother's approval, and still hoped to win it.* And each still feared her wrath and displeasure, because it was too painful and long-lasting to endure or attempt to battle. Before their conversions, both women had feared close or intimate friendships because of the conflicts they had grown up expecting to be part of "love." Though both had hated this dominating and devouring kind of love, they had to face the fact that the thing they hated most was a part of themselves.

I have never known more well-meaning women, nor women more anxious to do God's will than these, and therefore both quickly saw what had happened in them. A seed of a possessive and devouring love[21] (that which each had experienced with her own mother) had come up in themselves; and as it was carnal and even diabolical in nature, it was easily sexualized. In order to restore spiritual wholeness, the women had to confess the sin of inordinate love (a spiritual sin) and the lust (a sin of the body) that issued from it. The psychological healing needed was that of *separation of their identities from that of their mothers,* along with prayer for a full inner freedom from the bondages the maternal possessiveness and domination had wrought in them.

The need for psychological healing in such a case is no small one. Without it, the women were in danger of falling again, and they were painfully aware of this. Each, in fact, had since denied herself a close relationship with another woman because she feared another fall. In the meantime, their lives as Christians, as wives and mothers, suffered the tensions of these fears and of their need for insight into, and release from, their problem.

To minister such a healing as this, we invoke the Presence of the Lord, asking for His power and love to come in and enable us to discern, and then to break, the oppressing bondages that have kept the person bound emotionally and spiritually to another. There are different degrees to this problem, of course, but in some it is as though the soul is "possessed" by the soul of the mother. The prayer is much like one of exorcism, only it is for deliverance from the domination of the mother and her inroads into the very spirit and soul of the daughter. One said to me, "My mother has raped my mind." Another, "I can never get away from the presence of my mother, even though I am hundreds of miles from her." It is truly a terrible bondage.

In a case such as this, false guilt will usually need to be dealt with first. Otherwise the woman may resist (albeit unconsciously) the healing and will rather berate and accuse herself for her problems with her mother. With her is the vague and irrational false guilt of never having been able to please her mother, never being able to meet her expectations, never being able to "love her enough." Pity and sadness for the emptiness in her mother's life will sometimes be paralyzing emotions within the false guilt. In completely disallowing her mother's psychological manipulation she will need to be released from fears that she is being unchristian and unloving. This psychological manipulation is, after all, what she has grown up to think of as "love." She must be assured that it is only after she has accepted her freedom (a full severing of her identity from that of her mother's) that she will be able to love and relate to her mother aright—as a whole, secure person. Until then, there is a part of her which is yet immature, yet under the law of her mother, yet subject to being manipulated. At last assured, she will be prepared to accept her freedom from the subjectivity that keeps her from maturing in some vital part of her personality, if not the whole of it.

In the prayer for such a one's release, I usually ask them to see Jesus with the eyes of their hearts, to see Him on the cross, there taking into Himself the very pain and bondage they are now struggling with, as well as any unforgiveness or sin within their hearts. I ask them to stretch out their hands to Him and see the pain and darkness flow into His outstretched, nail-riven hands as I pray for the severance of their souls from the domination of their mother's. I often, without interrupting the rhythm of the prayer, softly ask them, "What are you seeing with the eyes of your heart?" And it is wonderful what they see as the darkness flows out of them and into Him. Often I will be seeing the same "picture" as the Holy Spirit leads the way.

Then, and I find this to be a very important step, I ask them to picture their mother. Because the Holy Spirit is in control and healing is so powerfully taking place, they will nearly always have a picture of her that is most revealing, one that will enable them to see her objectively for the first time, one that will better enable them to fully forgive her. Then I ask them to look and see if there are any bondages left between them. They will *see* it and *name* it. I then ask them, as though they had scissors in their hands, to cut through the bonds they see. The release that comes with this is often nothing short of phenomenal, and there are times when there are definite emotional and even physical reactions to the release. We will have seen these bonds sometimes as thick diseased umbilical cords, other times as threadlike ropes between the souls of the two, etc. When they are cut, we see a symbolic picture, one that is a true one, of the very deliverance that is taking place.

In a few extreme cases, when the psychological bondage has been particularly severe, or there has been occult and demonic power on the part of the mother, it was as though I had a sword in my hand, the very Sword of the Spirit, cutting bonds that looked like ropes from the very pits of Hell. After the naming and cutting of these bondages, I sometimes see in their hearts the now severed roots of these old bondages, and by prayer we pluck them out. We then see, as we pray, God's healing love flowing in, closing the wounds, making whole the heart.

When the need for the severance of one's identity from another is rightly discerned and prayed for, the healing can be well-nigh incredible. In the power of His Presence, the release into wholeness and freedom is complete; the joy of it is at times simply overwhelming. With it, one gains an objective stance from which to deal with the problems such a relationship presents, and this too can be awesome to the soul who has never before had the wholeness within that would allow such a stance. She can practice His Presence then, seeing herself standing alone though enveloped in His love and light.

Once healed, the two women in this story were able to receive the words that come from God, and were able to find continuing release from the old accusing voices of the world, the flesh, and the devil. Having been delivered from bondage to another's diseased love and will, both were free to make their wills absolutely one with God's. Free to listen to God, free to fully obey Him, these women were free to *become*. No longer hampered by guilt, false or real, they stepped into maturity with its wonderful gift of objectivity, and began to experience freedom of relationships not only with their mothers, but with all others as well. In their respective parts of their country, both are now effectively ministering to others in the Body of Christ.

Hellish Kinds of Counselors

I have seen instances where a lesbian relationship issues out of what begins as merely a "counseling" situation between one woman and another, and ends as an unholy wedding where each feeds the self-pitying illusion the other lives by. This can happen when the inner loneliness and tactile needs of someone (such as one suffering from infantile deprivation) come into collusion with another's need to shape, direct, "do things to,"[22] or otherwise control and dominate another soul.

Such a dominating personality is like the women in the previous story, only drastically different in that she is closed to any healing for herself and unwilling to submit to God's will. She also may be quite clever at hiding her manipulativeness, her possessiveness, her neediness. She then, though the stronger personality of the two, will even so be an equally neurotic one, but one without the tactile or sexual needs of the other woman. She will, however, as "counselor" in the situation, eventually sexualize their relationship in order to meet the needs she plainly perceives in the other.

The end of such a circumstance can be terrible for both the participants, as well as for any other soul unlucky enough to get caught in the crossfire such relationships generate. The children, the husbands, and the extended families suffer greatly in such circumstances as these, and as ministers we need to concentrate on helping them. Persons such as these, armed with the extreme feminist rhetoric of the day, are fully capable of projecting all their own guilt onto their husbands or others who seem to stand in their way. These hapless family members, unable to discern and deflect the irrationality of their arguments and behavior, will often think themselves to be losing their minds, will often complain of extreme mental and emotional confusion. With the prayer and ministry of others, they can be spared a breakdown and continue to be the responsible family member in the situation.

It is surprising how often these women seem to gain their priest's or minister's apologies for their behavior, and this on top of everything else will be more than the overburdened husband or family member can withstand. The rhetoric of the day, along with the absence of the power to heal, seems to take its toll even on the reasoning powers of some clergy. How much more, then, is the confusion of the layman, whose reasoning powers are untutored in the psychology of man and who has no theological and philosophical background with which to contrast and discern the false ideologies of the day.

Lesbian Behavior Connected with the Influence of the Father

There are (comparatively rare) times when a father, disappointed over the birth of an infant daughter, treats her as if she were the desired son. She is rewarded for copying him in dress, for following him in home repairs and carpentry projects, and in fishing with him in an all-masculine context. In these circumstances she can easily grow up to be aggressive with women, and masculine in her mannerisms. She then cannot readily accept the feminine role with a would-be suitor. There are times when such a one marries a man who accepts her highly developed masculinity, and the marriage in such a case can be surprisingly successful. When this more fortunate outcome is not the case, however, and she finds her loneliness alleviated only in the fellowship of other lonely women, she can have problems with sexual aggressiveness toward certain ones she posits her affection in. She, like Jay in an earlier story, has modeled herself after the wrong parent. She is separated from that part of her personality which was never affirmed by her father—her innate femininity.

It is more difficult for a woman to integrate with her estranged femininity than for a man (as in Jay's story) to find and integrate with his alienated masculinity. Perhaps it is because every man, unlike his sister, must separate his sexual identity from that of his mother, and it is more or less a natural task. I recently heard what was quoted as an old saying: "A man is not a man until his father *tells* him he is a man." That axiom holds in a nutshell what I've certainly seen to be a law at work between fathers and sons. But what of the little girl who has from her birth been called a man by her father? She who ordinarily would not have the task her brother has, that of separating her sexual identity from that of her mother's, now has the unnatural task of separating her sexual identity from that of her father. This explains, it seems to me, why her difficulty in integrating with her feminine self is such a difficult one and why the unconscious resistance to it is so great.

She needs healing for the very deep rejection she experienced, not of herself as a person, but of herself as a feminine sexual being. Prayer for this will include, of course, the forgiving of those who failed to accept or affirm her in her femininity. Any confession she should make in regard to lesbian activity, as well as any deliverance and absolution she might need, would also be part of this prayer. Then prayer should be directed toward the main psychological need she has, that of acknowledging and accepting her feminine self.

The prayer of faith will envision this estranged feminine self and see it being accepted and integrated into the personality. This is not hard to do. We have acknowledged the Presence of our Lord and we see with His eyes the beautiful woman within, waiting to be affirmed, to be called forward. These prayers are to be specific in their supplications, and the minister is to paint a verbal prayer picture of the needy one's acceptance of her innate feminine self, in whatever way the Holy Spirit leads, giving thanks that the integration is even now beginning to take place.

With this powerful help from the Lord, the woman can begin the process of *becoming*, of integrating with the feminine self she has so long denied. This healing comes under the heading of the third barrier to inner healing, that of failure to accept oneself. As we have seen, she must realize that her decision to accept herself is one that she alone can make. To teach such a one to listen to God is ever so important here, for she is to yield up to God all her old attitudinal patterns toward herself and receive in exchange the Lord's affirmation of her as a woman.

We are often very much afraid of the part of ourselves we are estranged from. Indeed, we are often afraid of the higher self *in toto* until we are enabled to accept it; until then we tend to run from it altogether. This tendency is wonderfully portrayed in Charles Williams's novel, *Descent into Hell*, by his heroine, Pauline Anstruther. She had "a certain thing of terror in her own secret life" and she had never considered the possibility that it was good. Since childhood she would occasionally see "herself coming towards herself," an apparition she dreaded so long as she ran from it. She became therefore very fearful of solitude, of being alone. It was only then that this thing of terror appeared, what she later learned was actually "a terrible good."

A wonderful analogy of the fact that a good and useful part of ourselves can at first appear horrifying and evil was just told me by a friend. It is the story of a wise old Sufi, his circulation sluggish, who lost the feeling in his right arm and shoulder as he slept. Awaking with a start, he reached with his left hand and felt what he thought to be a huge cold reptile next to his right side. On hearing his cry that there was a snake in his bed, his brothers brought a light into his cell, and he was found to be grasping his own right arm. To the woman we are discussing, her femininity is not only unimaginable, it is as alien and frightening to her as the old Sufi's right arm was when he thought he had hold of a serpent. By simply *seeing* and affirming the "woman within," we show it to be (though paralyzed within her) the "terrible good" that it truly is.

The task of accepting herself as a woman will be greatly speeded up if she can be persuaded of the importance of "putting on" her feminine self or image by dressing in an entirely different and feminine manner, as well as by deliberately adopting new and feminine mannerisms. Since she cannot imagine herself in this way, she will need (as Jay did) deliberately and prayerfully to select a model at first. The image, as any professional could tell us, really matters. One is a better banker when he *looks* like one, at least in the beginning. A woman is more feminine in blouses and flowing skirts than in jeans or overalls.

Perhaps we should look at this principle from a spiritual standpoint. St. Paul, calling us to inner Christlikeness, asks us to "put on Christ." The outer image or garb, as he well knew, stimulates the inner man in its becoming.[23] This is why the *practice* of the Presence of Christ is so very effective. This "exterior" putting on makes the Christian aware of the Christ who is more truly present to us, within and without, than any created entity or thing. This is true even at the psychological level. The woman who can put on her feminine self (even though she cannot herself sense it within) will find the exterior action stimulating the inner growth and maturation of her entire feminine being—emotional, intuitive, intellectual, and sensory.

The woman, of course, is to always have the fullest freedom of choice in this matter, as well as in any other. I speak of *persuading* only in the sense of an enthusiastic and joyful presentation of the woman I see within her, but that she is out of touch with, and of our sharing this vision with her. She is never to feel coercion. If the one who prays for her (or for anyone) strays from simply presenting the truth, and the way (in his opinion) that this truth can best be realized, and begins to manipulate in any way, that one has strayed from his healing vocation. Our Lord never transgressed a person's will. He did show them in every way possible the wholeness and the freedom he saw within them and that was their inheritance as the children of God.

Within this freedom is not only a continuing responsibility of choice, but the powerful privilege of taking authority over our own souls and bodies. One writer speaks of this authority we as Christians can have over our own lives, and in so doing addresses the principle under discussion:

> Authority with God discloses authority with the Self. The divine Self, the esse, lies quiescent, still, waiting in all men to be stirred into action by the outer self. Two kinds of address stir the still esse to action, viz., command and praise.[24]

It has been said in various ways by some great Christian spiritual directors of the past that the soul creates a body adequate to its use and reflecting its character. Most of us have noted that a slovenly soul presents a slovenly physical appearance, a rakish soul a rakish appearance. A woman, out of touch with her femininity and overly developed in her masculinity, will reflect this in her entire physical appearance. I believe that her dwarfed feminine self adversely affects all aspects of her life.

In this section I am of course not speaking of borderline cases. I am thinking, for example, of those such as the following I have ministered to: As far back as this woman's memory goes, she was dressed *only* as a male butcher to work alongside her butcher father. She slaughtered animals as a man would, dressed them as a man would, drank her beer as her German forefathers would, and was being prepared to run the family business as male ancestors had. She had no brother to do these things alongside her father, and though he loved her, her father affirmed her only as the son he wanted her to be.

She could in no way be convinced that her feminine self was a beautiful thing, and that it could be befriended. The fact that I could so clearly see it was meaningless to her. She had beautiful blue eyes and curly blonde hair that wisped in careless ringlets about her face. There was an incredibly beautiful woman hidden beneath the masculine bulk and mannerisms that made up her exterior image. She was unable to "put on" her femininity, and I was not to press the principle at this level, but simply to give thanks that she had been healed spiritually and to a great extent psychologically—i.e., she had experienced deliverance from lesbian lusts and compulsions and the healing of the rejection of herself as a woman. I was to rest comfortably knowing that she had "put on" Christ, and that this principle at work on the spiritual level, the highest of all, would begin the softening, freeing work she needed at the psychological level. Eventually, as she remained faithful in listening to her Lord, I knew that even her body would begin to reflect the fact that Christ is gathering all that she is into His completeness—a delicate and wonderful process.

Lesbian Behavior Connected with Hatred and/or Fear of Men

There are instances where lesbian behavior is connected to fear and hatred of the father or of some other man. Out of hatred any and every kind of perversion can come. Unhealed schisms, whether between the sexes, the races, classes of workers, rich and poor, young and old, always breed hatred and therefore always form breeding grounds for various perversions. Such a condition is exacerbated today (and in some cases even induced in the first place) by extremes in feminist political rhetoric that not only open the mind to hatred, but also to lesbian sexuality.

It is in forgiving others their trespasses (no matter how heinous), and in yielding up our own hatred, fear, and rebellion that we receive the gift of a new heart—one that is healed, softened, and freed. As ministers praying with a woman who has long held hatred and fear in her heart toward men, we would direct her to look up as we prayed and see Jesus with the eyes of her heart. This would be in contrast to any attempt on our part to induce some conscious frame of mind capable of forgiving. (See Johnny's story earlier in this chapter.)

On the other hand, the conscious reasoning mind needs ministry before the prayer begins in order that any intellectual barriers may be removed. Women, especially those caught up in the rhetoric of schism and hate, need the benefit of alternative perspectives. False or incomplete ideologies and perspectives need to be revealed as such, and this is not to be done in an attempt to change or coerce anyone's mind or power of choice. A statement of higher perspectives is what is needed and called for. The woman's heart is thus opened and enlarged to choose a way that will not only bring the freedom she seeks, but one that makes room for love.

During such a prayer, of course, there are times we appeal to one's conscious, reasoning mind in order to help them to forgive. At crucial moments, for example, when one comes right up to forgiving and then cries out, "I cannot forgive," I have found myself pointing at the irrationality of their hatred and fear and of the utterly irrational destruction it will continue to bring down upon them if they do not forgive. It has been my experience to then see them, after this appeal to their reason, *will* to forgive— a wonderful action of the rational mind that no doubt draws its strength from the depths of the heart as well.

The woman's hatred, that perhaps began with resentment toward her father or some other man, that then generalized to all males, causing her to be "schizoid" in relation to men, is thus yielded up to God, and the woman is released. This is no small healing and she, like others, will need to continue in the Presence of the Lord, there exchanging old diseased attitudinal patterns for the new ones He alone can build in. Patterns of love toward all, bondage to none—that is God's desire for each of us.

Tactile Needs in Lesbian Behavior

The consideration of tactile needs returns us to the prime category in lesbian behavior, that of the absence of mother-love in early infancy, or the inability to receive it when proffered. Sometimes the woman deprived to one extent or another of a mother's loving touch as an infant has tactile (touch) needs that are overwhelming, even compulsive. This points to the importance of nursing infants at the breast, of holding and caressing them. When this touch-love has been missing or inadequate, it is difficult to make up the difference later. The touch of others does not suffice for it, even as various other attempts to compensate do not. In fact, it takes the Lord's healing touch to make up for the deficit and free the woman from her attempts to compensate, a terrible condition that until surmounted will not allow her to go on to other concerns. Until this happens, she may think of herself primarily in sensory or sexual terms.

Those in whom the tactile needs are greatest will sometimes have a problem with overeating and with masturbation. Both habits will be attempts to compensate for unmet tactile needs, but will invariably end up a mixture of other things (such as lust and self-pity) as well. These problems will then militate against the thing the needy woman longs for most: a close physical relationship with a husband.

There are many women who suffer this deficit, and who also have the strong tactile needs to go with it, who would never involve themselves in lesbian sexuality. Sara's experience is a good example of this. Born the fifth child in a quick succession of babies, she was the infant of a worn-out, physically ill mother. Not only was Sara's mother without physical stamina, but she was also psychologically and spiritually depleted. She simply did not have the capacity for one more child in her arms or in her heart. Sara suffered keenly through all this, but did not go on to sexualize her identity as some do. In other words, Sara's strong tactile needs did not drive her to think of herself in primarily sexual terms. She simply needed healing of infantile memories of deprivation along with the courage to face her inner loneliness and invite God into it. But some, unlike Sara, go on to sexualize their identities, and their problems grow in complexity.

Tactile Needs and the Sexualized Identity

I have seen a number of cases where a woman's unmet need for fondling is exacerbated by some difficulty having to do with sex in her youth, and out of these circumstances she (though unconsciously) sexualizes her identity. She then comprehends what it means to be loved mostly in sensual or overtly sexual terms. This condition is greatly aggravated by the present permissive culture we live in, with its emphasis on sexual freedom and sexual fulfillment. Given the failure of a marital relationship to materialize, the groundwork is then laid within her personality for a fall into a lesbian relationship.

Lana's story is typical of this condition found in lesbian behavior. Besides the absence of mother-love and fondling, she was from a very early age sexually abused by her father's younger brother. As an adult, she had conflicting feelings about this sexual abuse because her need for touch was to some extent gratified in these sordid and degrading circumstances. She was at once ashamed of how her youthful uncle had treated her, and guilty for needing the touch, however perverse and unloving. These circumstances were enough to start her on the road to thinking of herself as primarily a sexual being and of receiving and giving love mostly in sensual terms. It should be emphasized that it does not take circumstances as extreme as incest to effect this in a woman; sometimes merely having parents whose problems revolve around sexual tensions can make this dimension of one's person seem to be the prime one.[25]

Lana's start in life was admittedly not very good, but a tendency toward self-pity and extreme selfishness didn't help her out any. She developed severe problems with masturbation and overeating. As time passed, her interpersonal relationships grew quite complicated. She became skillful in the manipulation of others in an attempt to get her own way.

When her various problems discouraged prospective husbands, she began to develop intense relationships with women, and finally, proclaiming herself to be "bisexual," she entered into a series of lesbian affairs. These relationships turned out to be hellish things indeed, and I first saw her for prayer and counseling after they had exploded into problems that upset not only her, but the quiet in several families and churches as well.

She was hurting badly, and needed healing for the old rejections and deprivations; she needed to realize she had sexualized her identity; she needed to know there was another way besides manipulation of people to alleviate the inner pain of loneliness and emptiness. We made a good beginning when she found out she could not manipulate me. I had to face her with her chief problem, that of having descended, with the help of self-pity and a self-centeredness that was quite repugnant, far down into the hell of self. I had to face her with what by now loomed large behind her problem with masturbation and also her lesbian activity. She had a perverse rationale under which she operated and even came close to verbalizing. It went like this: "Look! I have needs. I deserve to have them met; if I don't get them met this way (through masturbation and lesbian behavior), no one else will help me!"

Along with this governing idea were accusations and anger, mostly below levels of conscious awareness, against both God and man. She paraded her lesbian relationship with each successive woman as "a real relationship, one of real love," but she had to look at all her activity and realize it to be the wholly pernicious and self-serving thing that it in truth was. She had to face the fact that her preoccupation with her own self and her own needs worked against her chances of ever being able to come into right relationships with either friends or the husband she longed to have. She had to know that until all this was confessed, turned from, and healed, she would destroy every relationship by trying to get her "needs" met.

"Love is something more stern and splendid than mere kindness," as C. S. Lewis has said, and the most unloving thing I could possibly have done to her would have been to substitute some sort of mindless "loving acceptance" for the very things that were killing her. It is one thing to accept a person where he or she is, and another to accept their malignant behavior that works against them as well as others. It is also one thing to accept the *real* person who stands before you needing to be freed, and another to accept (and direct a kindly tolerance toward) his or her old carnal self who dons whatever "face" the occasion might call for while preventing the real, creative self from coming forward. Jesus Christ never wasted His time, energy, and prayer by helping a person "practice the presence" of the old carnal self. He didn't converse with it, or exercise the great virtue of kindness toward it. He paid attention to it only by saying, "Die to it!"

The practice of the Presence of Jesus is vital on the part of one who would minister healing in His name. In practicing His Presence (*within* myself as well as without and all about), I also pray to see those I minister to through His eyes, and His eyes alone. Through years of doing this, I am convinced that He so loves and concentrates on freeing the real person that He hardly sees the old illusory one once it has been discerned and named as the usurper it is. Rather, His lovingkindness blazes out in healing light toward the *real person* He created.

In Lana I could see the real self struggling to come up and out from under layers of the self-centered, self-pitying, carnal old nature. I appealed to the real Lana and called her to come up out of the hell of self in Jesus' name. This is exactly what began to take place, and after several more sessions we were ready to pray for the healing of the old memories of rejection and deprivation. Today her life is altogether different. Because her identity is no longer sexualized, her intellectual, imaginative, and spiritual horizons have appeared and continued to expand. As a child of God, she realizes that "the Christian has still to work, with mind as well as body, to suffer, hope and die."[26] In other words, life is always a struggle and heroism is essential for victory. Yet she now sees unlimited possibilities of *becoming* and knows herself to be in harmony with them. She now perceives that all her "bents and faculties have a purpose"[27] and are being redeemed.

For some time she wanted to continue to receive her help through me or another Christian, rather than develop the necessary vertical relationship to God. I had strongly to exhort and teach her to listen to God for herself, and to set aside a period of solitude and quiet with Him each day. This was an absolute necessity if her real self was to come fully forward and mature and blossom. It was also the key to helping her overcome the last vestige of self-pity, and the habits of masturbation and overeating that accompanied it.

Each one of us, not just the ones with early deprivations such as Lana and the others suffered, has to gain the courage and determination to face the inner loneliness and *there* begin to hear God and our own truest selves. The necessity to do this is only the more urgent for the Lanas and the Lisas. In Henri Nouwen's wonderful imagery, we must convert the "desert of loneliness" deep within each of us into a "garden of solitude" where spiritual life begins and blossoms. "Instead of running away from our loneliness and trying to forget or deny it, we have to protect it and turn it into a fruitful solitude."[28] This is a vital part of what it means to practice the Presence, of what it means to come into that vertical relationship to God.

Lana's strongest inclination was to avoid facing her own inner loneliness, and indeed to fear it. To fear and run from it was to fear and run from her true self. She had to learn (through dogged discipline at first) to *protect* the very thing she had always feared the most, her own loneliness, and to find that it was indeed "hiding unknown beauty."[29] In His Presence she would grow emotionally as well as intellectually and spiritually. It was my part to insist on and lead the way into this spiritual discipline.

Removing Ugly Pictures from the Memory Bank

Nearly always a married woman who has had lesbian experience needs this healing, a wonderful one and very simple to pray for.

Time and again such a woman will be sent to me, perhaps by her priest or counselor, and she will say, "When my husband starts to make love to me, these awful pictures come into my mind. I simply freeze. When I came to Jesus, he forgave me, I know, but I am so frightened. These pictures are ruining my relationship with my husband."

The deep mind is both like and unlike a computer. It holds every memory, forgetting not a single one, while at the same time (unlike the computer) it holds not only the fact, but the vivid *pictures* of those memories as well. When one has become a Christian, and he or she starts to pray, gets quiet, or gets into a situation where he is reminded of the old condition, these old pictures attempt to come up. The Christian, thinking "This cannot be!" simply thrusts them right back down, rather like ramming the lid down quickly on a garbage can.

The pictures, of course, that are coming into the woman's mind are those of her forsaken lesbian activity. She has now been forgiven and set free from the activity, but she needs to yield up the old pictures that have been programmed into the heart's computer.

We go to prayer and I ask her to look and see Jesus with the eyes of her heart and stretch out her opened hands to receive from Him. After a little preliminary prayer, I ask Jesus to bring up every bad or fearful picture from her heart and mind; and as I pray, this is exactly what He does. They come up one at a time. I ask her to reach her hand to her forehead and take each one as it comes up from her mind, and then hand it to Jesus, whose outstretched hands she visualizes.

This doesn't take long, and always heals the problem. After the last one has come up, I ask her to look and see what Jesus is doing with the old pictures. She sees Him do away with them in the way most meaningful to her. I then pray that His love and light enter into her, filling all those spaces where the old pictures of a diseased form of sexual activity and lovemaking had been. The problem is now outside her, so to speak, and she can withstand any Satanic attempt to reprogram the picture-making faculty of the deep mind.

I have learned to pray this prayer for groups before taking them on an "imaginary journey," something I frequently do as an exercise of *freeing the heart to see* any pictures God would send before prayer for healing of memories. Otherwise, those with repressed fearful and/or pornographic pictures will have them pop up during the beautiful journey. Some people are afraid to pray or meditate because when they do, these pictures erupt. They too need this very simple healing.

Homosexual and Lesbian Behavior Related to Failure of the Infant to Achieve an Adequate Sense of Being

The identity problem in this group is severest of all, for the sufferer experiences to one degree or another the separation from the sense of *being* itself. Up to now we have talked about those parts of ourselves we are separated from and cannot accept: our masculinity, our femininity, our physical appearance, our good minds or whatever. But in this, the trauma has been such that a sense of being itself is either extremely tenuous or missing altogether. Sometimes, because this trauma by no means always manifests itself in homosexual behavior, the sufferer will posit his identity in an object or fetish. At other times, he or she will simply suffer an aloneness and a mental and emotional pain beyond what the ordinary person can even imagine. When such a sufferer chooses the homosexual route to alleviate this painful sense of nonbeing, it is an hysterical[30] attempt to find his missing being or to posit his very frail sense of being and identity in another person.

This most critical category is one then that simply reflects to a greater degree the psychological traumas human babies can suffer when either the love and care they need to realize themselves as persons in their own right is missing, or some injury or grievous circumstance has rendered them unable to receive the mother's love and care at a meaningful level. These sufferers, because of the severity of their needs, often appear in the minister's study with long and complicated medical histories, and are sometimes labeled as schizoid, hysterical, or even schizophrenic personalities by their doctors.

I am indebted to Dr. Frank Lake, an English psychiatrist-theologian and onetime missionary to India, for some of the terminology I'll use in this chapter. As a depth-psychologist, he has done extensive research into early psychological injuries, at first using drugs and hypnosis to abreact (bring up) these early experiences in his most critically ill homosexual patients. His findings coincide with and scientifically affirm what we find in prayer for healing of memories. In fact, Dr. Lake himself has now learned to abreact these memories through prayer alone, and he no longer uses either hypnosis or drugs to enable his patients to relive the deeply submerged root trauma. For a psychological and spiritual understanding of this group of homosexual sufferers, as well as for the needed pastoral insights into hysterical behavior, I recommend his book, *Clinical Theology.*[31]

Mental pain, Dr. Lake says, is essentially separation-anxiety, and has its roots in the trauma of some rejection experienced in early infancy. This has happened before the infant knows itself to be separate from its source of being, its mother. The love shining through her eyes, Dr. Lake says, becomes the umbilical cord through which it derives its sense of being. The loss of the mother or the mother substitute, through sickness, death, desertion, or simply through suffering her absence in a period of great stress, can result in the infant's failure to (1) achieve a sense of well-being, or (2) of being itself. The latter results in an identification with nonbeing.

There are physical as well as psychological injuries that can render a baby unable to relate to its mother and thereby receive in the glow of her love its own healthy sense of being. Birth traumas that leave a baby wanting to recede into itself and back into the womb are not infrequent. In the severest cases, anything outside the womb, including the mother, is rejected. The term *separation-anxiety* takes on tremendous meaning after one has seen the abreaction of infantile memories such as these. Everything I've ever learned through prayer for healing of memories confirms the truth of what Dr. Lake declares in the following paragraphs:

> Neurotic anxiety and the irrational fears and pains into which it translates itself are not the direct result of unhappy circumstances in the present. The mental pain of a breakdown is the echo of the pain of long-lost relationships. The echo resonates through into consciousness because a painful loneliness has descended again upon the person. . . . Neurotic anxiety is the addition to that reasonable fear of strange, unreasonable terrors, that is, of the long-repressed separation-anxieties of infancy. . . . The buried past turns a tolerably fearful present moment into an intolerably anxious one.[32]
>
> The roots of all the psychoneuroses lie in infantile experiences of mental pain of such an intolerable severity as to require splitting off from consciousness at about the time they occurred. These have remained buried by repression. The actual cause of the panic may be a time of separation-anxiety endured during the early months of life, when to be separated from the sight and sensory perception of the source of "being," in mother or her substitute, is tantamount to a slow strangling of the spirit and its impending death. The various patterns of the psychoneuroses comprise and indicate a variety of defences against this separation.[33]

When Homosexual Behavior Forms Part of the Defense

Homosexual behavior is but one of these defenses. Dr. Lake says there are two types of homosexuality related to separation-anxiety: the one associated with the loss of well-being, and the other, which is infinitely worse, that associated with the loss of *being* itself. I think that Matthew's condition (Chapter 3) included this most difficult injury in at least the loss of well-being.

Dr. Lake tells of numerous cases of homosexual patients who relive (by abreaction under drugs) a traumatic or painful period of babyhood in which life in the woman's care has been horrific and the condition of separation-anxiety has been the result. The baby has been thrust over a threshold into a schizoid position of dread in which the basic fear is that of identification with non-being.

The schizoid position is synonymous, in Dr. Lake's use of the term, with an experience of unbearable dread, of a fall into disrelatedness, or of identification with nonbeing. The baby boy, suffering such a trauma before six months of age, is then "schizoid" in respect to his mother. In her hands, for whatever reason, he did not come to a sense of well-being or even of being itself—and she is therefore associated with this terrible dread. This association is then generalized to all other women. He becomes male-centered. He may then form a hysterical attachment to a man. The psychodynamics of the hysterical personality are revealed in a clinging attachment to things or to the person in whom he or she is finding, or attempting to find, his or her identity.

The baby girl reacts differently than the baby boy in that she, when suffering this same injury (that of being unable to gain a sense of well-being, or even of being itself, in the love of her mother or mother substitute) enters the hysterical rather than the schizoid position in regard to women.

> The hysterical reaction to the impending loss of life-by-relatedness to the mother is the root experience tending to lesbian homosexuality in baby girls, rather than boys. The boy who remains hysterically attached to mother figures may manage to transfer his fixation to the woman whom he marries, to whom he looks for mothering as well as for everything else. The girl to whom this happens may transfer her fixed need for dependence on the mother figure to another woman.[34]

All who know anything of ministry to those with this condition will agree that it is truly a terrible burden to carry in this life.

The psychological healing of this, "the most terrible deprivation known to the mind of man, that of a mother's love withdrawn from the baby," is not painless, nor by any stretch of the imagination easy, for it requires a facing up to the inner loneliness and emptiness that some of these sufferers have spent a lifetime running away from.[35] Every ounce of strength has been used to repress rather than face the spectres rising out of this "terrible abyss of nonbeing." One can understand how it would seem inborn (a genetic condition) to those whose presuppositions and methodologies do not allow for early infantile trauma, for the condition of these sufferers seems *always* to have been. This androcentric pattern appears to have come with the baby.

Their need is the same in one sense, only much more pronounced, as it is for all of us fallen persons: that of courageously facing the inner emptiness and crying out to the only One who can complete and heal us. They receive their healing in exactly the same way as others described in this book. The one who prays and works with them, however, is deeply conscious of the almost unimaginable dimensions of the healing that is needed. Such a sufferer, like all the others, must cling to the cross (with all that means) until he forgives the very circumstances of his life and gains Christ's forgiving and healing *grace*. This grace enables him to yield up his suffering, along with all the deep-rooted rage and anger, into the hands of the Crucified One. In this grace, he sees *why* Christ died—to take this very pain. He sees that Christ has suffered this burden all along, and he has only to give it fully to Him. He sees that Christ not only became man and took upon Himself our suffering, but that *He became sin for us*. He who is love *became*, as the sacrificial Lamb of God, the terrible sin of unlove that left us so injured.

In prayer, we see Him on the cross, and we take our place in His crucified body. We actually see this with the eyes of our heart as the spiritual reality is taking place. Then we see even our failure to achieve a sense of being, our horrific fear of falling into the abyss of nonbeing, taken up into His greater *Being* and sacrifice.

> We have confidence to enter the Most Holy Place by the blood of Jesus, by a new and living way opened for us through the curtain, that is, his body.[36]

We pass through "the curtain, that is, his body," dying to the old diseased forms of love we have clung to as well as to the unspeakable loneliness and pain of being *disrelated* at this most basic of all levels. Forgiving others as well as all the circumstances of our lives, we rise with Him in newness of life. Born anew, we take our place in His resurrected Being. In the cross there is healing; in His resurrected body and life there is *identity* and *being*.

Here are excerpts from one who suffered this severest injury and had attempted to assuage the unbearable pain of the failure to achieve a sense of being in a mother's love through fearfully concealed lesbian relationships. The awe of her healing was still with her as she wrote,

> How I rejoice this morning in a very deep and quiet way about New Year's Eve. I went to the communion rail to receive Jesus' body and blood. His presence was vivid and He knew I didn't want to rush. Just as the lay reader came to me there was no consecrated wine left, so I gently waited with Him while Fr. S consecrated more. Then I received His blood. The Presence was so real. . . . As I crawled into bed this morning [after the Midnight Mass] the thought came to me that it was not since [20 yrs. before] that I had been at the Lord's table on New Year's Eve. Marveling at His healing and His protection through the years, I slept in peace.

Two Scriptures began to minister to her, the first from 2 Corinthians 5:17—"Therefore, if anyone is in Christ, he is a new creation; the old has gone, the new has come." The second was verse 18: "All this is from God, who reconciled us to himself through Christ, and gave us the ministry of reconciliation." "Reconciliation," she writes, "what a word with which to start His new decade!"

One would need to know the extent of her inner desert of deprivation to appreciate the fact that a lifetime of the severest separation-anxiety and its effects is being swallowed up in the peace and joy she knows in her oneness with Christ.

> Since [the evening] when you, [Miss A.] and I prayed in the chapel, and Jesus Christ entered me and every cell of my body, His Presence has been constant and my spirit is recognizing more and more the Father, Son and Holy Spirit. I clearly remember you saying more than once we must practice the Presence. Praise God, it has been 10 months since that time of prayer and His reality has continued to grow within me.

I shall never forget the haunting years of pain and need that were written in this young woman's face as she sat in a seminar I was teaching, nor her astonishment when she began realizing that perhaps, after all the years of seeking help, there just might be help for her. A dreadful agony accompanied her astonishment, because she simply couldn't bear to experience hope and then see it dashed. She fired question after question at me, revealing that her search for wholeness had led her down many intellectual and theological paths.

> Before you prayed with me, I prayed to God not to let me experience a high, for I knew how low I could fall. Instead I asked for *depth*. Last night I thanked Jesus for not only answering that prayer, but for continuing to honor it. . . . Believe me, I am not talking about creampuff experience, for there have been times when I have cried in agony, sobbed with joy, run ahead of Him and lagged behind. But firmly, tenderly and gently Jesus has been teaching me through His Word, through prayer, and through Miss A. (and I thank God that she is such a clear, uncluttered channel for the work of the Holy Spirit), and through Fr.   . . . . Time and energy do not permit me to relate many events of these last

eight months, but then you know God's handiwork and you would not be surprised—in my awe I am still surprised and find myself with my jaw dropping in amazement (Luke 1:37— "For nothing is impossible with God").

She ends her letter with thanks and praise to God for the love she now knows and that is continually renewed within her being. Fullness of *being*—that is glory, and this she now possesses. This is the heritage available to all God's children in Jesus Christ.

A priest whose homosexuality was associated with this severest injury writes to me a poem about his experience of entering into Christ's death and finding his healing there. One line images the hands of the Crucified, reaching out, "putting death to death in me." I know of no finer way to describe the healing of one who never in his mother's arms reached a sense of being.

This is the heritage of those who choose union with Christ and a listening communion with Him. This union, designed by God Himself for the healing of the world, is in absolute contrast to the unnatural sexual union of one person with a member of his or her own sex—the remedy homosexual apologists urge upon such a sufferer today as a means of physical satisfaction of homosexual desires. These very desires, as we have seen, are indeed merely part of "a symbolic confusion," one that with the help of God can be cleared up.

"Alleluia All My Gashes Cry"[37]

Even before the psychological healing comes (as well as after), God can turn such wounds in this "severest category" into healing power. "Every disability," as C. S. Lewis realizes, "conceals a vocation." His understanding of this in relation to the homosexual condition is revealed in the following letter he wrote to Sheldon Vanauken:

I have seen less than you but more than I wanted of this

terrible problem. I will discuss your letter with those whom I think wise in Christ. This is only an *interim* report. First, to map out the boundaries within which all discussion must go on, I take it for certain that the *physical* satisfaction of homosexual desires is sin. This leaves the homosexual no worse off than any normal person who is, for whatever reason, prevented from marrying. Second, our speculations on the cause of the abnormality are not what matters and we must be content with ignorance. The disciples were not told *why* (in terms of efficient cause) the man was born blind (Jn. 9:1-3): only the final cause, that the works of God should be made manifest in him. This suggests that in homosexuality, as in every other tribulation, those works can be made manifest: i.e., that every disability conceals a vocation, if only we can find it, which will "turn the necessity to glorious gain." Of course, the first step must be to accept any privations which, if so disabled, we can't lawfully get. The homosexual has to accept sexual abstinence just as the poor man has to forego otherwise lawful pleasures because he would be unjust to his wife and children if he took them. That is merely a negative condition. What should the positive life of the homosexual be? I wish I had a letter which a pious male homosexual, now dead, once wrote to me—but of course it was the sort of letter one takes care to destroy. He believed that his necessity *could* be turned to spiritual gain: that there were certain kinds of sympathy and understanding, a certain social role which mere *men* and mere *women* could not give. But it is all horribly vague—too long ago. Perhaps any homosexual who humbly accepts his cross and puts himself under Divine guidance will, however, be shown the way. I am sure that any attempt to evade it (e.g., by mock- or quasi-marriage with a member of one's own sex *even* if this does not lead to any carnal act) is the wrong way. Jealousy (this another homosexual admitted to me) is far more rampant and deadly among them than among us. And I don't think little concessions like wearing the clothes of the other sex in private is the right line either. It is the duties, the burdens, the characteristic virtues of the other sex, I expect, which the patient must try to cultivate. I have mentioned humility because male homosexuals (I don't know about women) are apt, the moment they find you don't treat them with horror and contempt, to rush to the opposite pole and start implying that they are somehow superior to the normal type. I wish I could be more definite. All I have really said is that, like all other tribulations, it must be offered to God and His guidance how to use it must be sought.[38]

There are many such as Lewis spoke of who have found a total spiritual healing by accepting the "psychological disablement even as the physically maimed or disabled must," and have put their hand securely in God's knowing that He will turn even this most terrible suffering to a most profound good. Dr. Lake speaks of three such persons:

> On three occasions of crisis in my own spiritual life in which I have had urgent need of spiritual help it has come to me from clergymen who were manifestly carrying this burden. Yet in another sense they had ceased to carry it as a burden. They had surmounted their limitations and the life of Christ in them carried both them and me. They were in the act of dying to the old self; in some cases even the pain seemed to be purged away, but not the fact of having suffered.[39]

Dr. Lake states that these are the ones to whom doctors in general have nothing hopeful to offer. But, he declares, we in the Church have the answer and the "therapy" for homosexual men and women. "There are many possible aspects of clergy training a man can afford to overlook, but not his responsibility to understand and treat homosexuality."[40]

The Hysterical Personality

There are many reasons for fearing to counsel and pray with persons whose homosexual condition is related to separation-anxiety in its severest forms and in whom hysterical personality traits are prominent. No novice in medicine or prayer will in such a case come out unscathed. Though many, such as the clergymen to whom Dr. Frank Lake referred, have suffered this alienation and allowed Christ to turn the dread desert terrain in their deep mind and heart into a fruitful garden of healing both for themselves and for others, there are others who have fallen further and further into the hysterical and schizoid positions. Those who pray will be careful never to label a person as hysterical or schizoid. For one thing, even psychiatrists and psychologists are cautious in pinning such a label on or using it when they do; for another, we in the healing ministry know how dangerous labels can be. It is a way of over-identifying with the problem, and under-identifying with the real person as Jesus sees him. But I find I must say something about the hysterical personality as such in order to give guidance to those who pray for healing of memories.

Hysterical traits are found in all of us, for we all have sinned and come short of the Kingdom of God. In other words, we have failed to always "live and move and find our being in God," and in Him alone. We have attempted rather to find our identity in and cling to someone or something other than our Creator and sustainer. A hysterical personality is one who exhibits these traits to an extreme and uncommon degree. A full-blown hysterical personality might, if he or she could ever honestly verbalize and express his feelings, say something like this to his counselor: "As long as I hold your attention, I am, I exist; my identity is in you at this moment. I look to you for my very being. I demand it of you. I feel as though there is nothing inside me, and I know that no one could ever love me. Therefore, I must hold you in this way—by your attention—or perhaps sexually if that fails. I must hold you any way I can." And this behavior can continue *ad infinitum,* and it usually does, *until the minister gets close to the real problem—that severe separation-anxiety and sense of non-being within the sufferer.*

It has been said that the difference between a more brilliant psychiatrist and a less skillful one is that the brilliant man recognizes the hysteric sooner and runs away faster. This is no idle jibe. The special demands of hysterical patients upon those who try to help them can become so like the tentacles of an octopus as to cause breakdowns among the medical and nursing staffs who have the misfortune to become unwisely involved. [41]

Unwary clergy and prayer counselors can and do fall, perhaps oftener and harder than do medical personnel. It takes only one mishandled hysteric to destroy the order and calm in a church while perhaps sexually or otherwise seriously seducing even the minister and other counselors in the process. The naive and the spiritually immature will be hit so hard and so fast they will hardly know what has happened to them.

Important to the ministry of prayer for healing of memories is the fact that hysterical traits are defense mechanisms against *insight,* insight into the real problem, the "abyss of nonbeing." Nothing brings this insight quicker than prayer for healing of memories. An hysteric can ask for prayer or spiritual guidance and come expecting merely to talk, and by that means to get the attention he both needs and craves. He will "hang in there," so to speak, with the counselor who only listens, but every defense mechanism he has ever developed will come into play the moment the one gifted in prayer for healing gets close to the chasm of loneliness in the depths of his being. Many (certainly not all) of these persons will run very fast from precisely the ones who can bring them to, and help them face, the terrible dread at the core of their beings.

For this reason I make the following recommendations and warnings to pastors and all who pray for the healing of these sufferers:

1. *Timing* is of the utmost importance in prayer for such a

sufferer. We do what we hear the Lord say—that is, as the Spirit of God leads—and not as some other well-meaning soul urges. Persons with this injury occasionally appear in my missions and even in Schools of Pastoral Care. If they are able to sit through the Spirit's probing during the meetings, and the insight that begins to come as the lectures proceed, they are usually ready to face the inner trauma. They are already beginning to forsake the hysterical horizontal relationship to another creature, and are beginning to straighten up into a vertical relationship to God, their Creator. Then, even though they have hysterical homosexual or lesbian relationships in their background or even now, they are—in their decision to face the inner loneliness—ready for healing.

Warning: Timing is of key importance. Do not pray with an hysteric because someone has urged him or her to come to you. You will end up part of his almost diabolically clever mechanism for getting the attention he needs and craves.

2. *Control of the situation* is also of utmost importance. The counselor must have always and ever the upper hand. "Love is something more splendid than mere kindness." He must know the stern love of God, and allow it to flow through him. Any weakness toward replacing God's love with the human loves and compassions will lose the battle before it begins. Again, the full-blown hysteric is almost diabolically clever in his or her attempts to gain the upper hand, in his attempts to get the attention he needs through manipulation of others. The counselor must be absolutely ready to see the sufferer go from him rather than weaken. And this is the loving thing to do. It prepares the way for the person's healing on down the road. As long as there is one counselor or pastor that can be manipulated, indeed, one member of the family, such a sufferer will not face the inner trauma. As Dr. Lake states, the counselor must decline the "confidante role," must say "No" to unreasonable de-

mands from the very beginning, must never be manipulated by threats of suicide, nor motivated by the emotional needs of the sufferer.

3. "The hysterical person's resistance to insight will almost certainly make her mishear what we have said and report it erroneously."[42] Those who pray with such sufferers as these, especially unwary young pastors and others who feel an obligation to see any and everyone urged upon them by the equally unwary, often find that their very best efforts and words have been misused, misquoted, and that their counselee has made everyone within a radius of miles around think black is white and white is black in regard to himself. The counselee may have brought down the wrath of elders, and even of a lawyer and judge, upon his head. In respect to homosexual hysterics, it may be the head of some homosexual apologist's group or even the Civil Liberties Union. In such a case, the counselor has made the mistake of getting too close to the real problem before the sufferer was ready to face it.

4. Prayer and ministry to the family rather than to the sufferer himself is often what we are primarily called to. Nearly always they will need it *during* ministry to such a one. They have been severely manipulated, made to think their very best efforts and motives are evil. Often they will say, "I think I am losing my mind. He/she has made me feel that right is wrong, and that wrong is right. I am so confused that I do not know what is right or what is good anymore." We need to free them from the bondage that like an evil net entraps them physically, mentally, and spiritually. Their feet, like the sufferer's, are caught in the darkest kinds of confusion. Their actions are ordinarily helplessly subjective, and embroil them ever further in the confusion.

5. Men are the most often fooled by these sufferers. Women

seem to have an intuitive knowledge beyond men in regard to the dangers such a one presents. Male pastors and counselors will do well to pay attention to their wives and to trusted and wise Christian women in their congregations.

6. When I am led to work with one like this, I enlist the aid of others who are in spiritual authority over him or her. Sometimes it will be his bishop, nearly always his priest or minister, and together we pray for this healing before I see the person. I also ask for aid, in cases where it is possible and plausible, from their psychiatrists and physicians, and confer with them. Under ordinary circumstances, I ask to do this with the permission of the sufferer and/or his family.

7. These people come into the fullest joy and wholeness as they come (usually slowly) into relationship with the individual members of the Body of Christ, something that would never have been possible before, but is possible and very necessary after their healing begins. Also, they will need spiritual guidance by someone who is an "uncluttered channel" for the Holy Spirit's continued "therapy" in their lives.

God Never Fails Such a Sufferer

It is a wonderful thing to be able to assure any such sufferer that his/her healing will come once he or she comes obediently into the Presence. This joyful assurance I always stress because his pain is such that he usually cannot see the healing light at the end of the tunnel. God never fails, and what a wonderful thing to be able to declare it. Dr. Lake knows and declares this same marvelous truth:

There is nothing in the hystero-schizoid makeup of the androcentric man or woman which limits the action of God upon the soul. Rather, since infinite attachment and infinite detachment are already present in such souls, they have, even on the human level, a premonition of the dimensions of the abyss over which Christ was stretched upon the Cross.[43]

Jesus is the great physician of the soul and if we who live and move and find our being in Him do not do this work, it is very safe to say that it will not be done. In His Presence with us are all the healing gifts of the Spirit. We have been wondrously empowered to do all that He has asked us to do, even to heal in His name. In this commission we must all labor together.

Five

The Identity Crisis According to the Scriptures

It is in Christ that the complete being of the Godhead dwells embodied, and in him you have been brought to completion.[1]

Personality is not a datum from which we start.[2] —C. S. Lewis

We are *becoming* persons. You are not who you will be. I am not, by the grace of God, who I will be. "You are Simon, John's son," Christ said to a bumbling fisherman whose identity perhaps lay in his ability to catch fish and in the bigness of his masculine person. But on Simon's confession of Jesus as Messiah, the Son of the living God, Christ pointed to his higher identity: "You are Peter, the Rock."[3] There is nothing more certain than that Peter was genuinely unable to see himself as Christ saw him— the man he was destined to *be* when fully mature and wholly functioning in the authority and love of God. Knowing this, Christ said to him, even as He says to each one of us, words to this effect: Follow Me; continue in My Presence and I will show you—as you choose to make your will one with Mine—who you really are and what you were born to do.

Simon will have to die to the old sin-dominated self—that self which is in union with the old Adam—and he will also have to do some thorough dying to who he thinks himself to be. Until he dies to the old inner vision of himself as well as to the principle of evil in his members, Christ's words shall continue to come to him as a personal shock: "Anyone who wishes to be a follower of mine must leave self behind; he must take up his cross, and come with me." Equally as electrifying, he will continue to see Christ point away from the old Simon he yet perceives himself to be and to the new Peter he as yet cannot see, and will hear Him ask: "What does a man gain by winning the whole world at the cost of his true self?"[4]

When we first *will* to follow—first attempt obedience[5]—God becomes not just some vague force, but very personal. Our idea of Him changes. Then, as He points to the deeps of our personalities, deeps both good and bad that we are not in touch with, our idea about ourselves changes. We find that we do not know ourselves very well. Herein is both the identity crisis and its cure. As we will to be *in Him*, He gathers together the scattered parts of ourselves we have been separated from.

Though this is the key to the healing of us all, this truth is perhaps seen most dramatically in the healing of the homosexual, for his struggle toward wholeness is always associated (as we have seen) with deep problems of personal identity. A secure sexual identity is merely part of a secure personal identity—one that spans the full range of what it means to be a human being.

I once heard a wise and scholarly man say, "If we know ourselves at all, it is with the greatest of difficulty." He spoke the truth. To know ourselves at all is to begin to be healed of the effects of the Fall, for it involves coming into a listening-speaking relationship to God. It is to recapture at least to some extent the Edenic situation. It is to realize more perfectly our union and communion with God. No small thing, indeed, but it is our inheritance (and a neglected one) as Christians. It is the healing of our primal loneliness.

"We are born helpless. As soon as we are fully conscious we discover loneliness," as C. S. Lewis has said.[6] Born lonely, we try hard to fit in, to *be* the kind of person that will cause others to like us. Craving and needing very much the affirmation of others, we compromise, put on any face, or many faces; we do even those things we do not like to do in order to fit in.[7] We are bent (to use Lewis's imagery) toward the creature, attempting to find our identity in him. Slowly and compulsively the false self closes its hard, brittle shell around us, and our loneliness remains.

One of the principal names for our God is *Elohim*, and we find Him thus referred to 2,701 times in the Scriptures. Elohim, a Hebrew word, indicates the relation of God to man as Creator. The healing of man—and his loneliness—has to do with acknowledging himself to be a creature, *created*, and in looking up and away from himself, from self-worship to the worship of Elohim, Creator of all that is: time, space, mass, myself. It is in this worship that our one true face appears, displacing the old false faces. It is in this honest and open speaking relationship that our true self bursts forth, cracking the shell of the old false self; and our old bondages and compulsions fall away with it.

But man would be God. Every inclination of his will, therefore, tends toward self-consciousness and flees from the God who is calling him into dialogue with Himself—into God-consciousness. Thus, from worshiping God as Creator, man worships himself, the creature. Homosexual behavior is merely one of the twisted paths this basic fallen condition in man takes. Truly, to write of the healing of the homosexual is to write of the healing of all men everywhere. We are all fallen, and until we find ourselves in Him, we thrust about for identity in the creature, the created.

All men, says St. Paul, not just those who, like Jews and Christians, have access to the Scriptures, can know and acknowledge Elohim by what He has created:

For all that may be known of God by men lies plain before their eyes; indeed God himself has disclosed it to them. His invisible attributes, that is to say his everlasting power and deity, have been visible, ever since the world began, to the eye of reason, in the things he has made. There is therefore no possible defence for their conduct; knowing God, they have refused to honour him as God, or to render him thanks. Hence all their thinking has ended in futility, and their misguided minds are plunged in darkness. They boast of their wisdom, but they have made fools of themselves, exchanging the splendour of immortal God for an image shaped like mortal man, even for images like birds, beasts, and creeping things. For this reason God has given them up to the vileness of their own desires, and the consequent degradation of their bodies, because they have bartered away the true God for a false one, and have offered reverence and worship to created things instead of to the Creator, who is blessed for ever; amen.[8]

In worshiping the creature, we lose our identity. St. Paul speaks of homosexual behavior because, it seems to me, the identity crisis is simply most clearly seen in it. We are all given over to base things, and we even find our identity in them.

When Gentiles who do not possess the law carry out its precepts by the light of nature, then, although they have no law, they are their own law, for they display the effect of the law inscribed on their hearts. Their conscience is called as witness, and their own thoughts argue the case on either side, against them or even for them, on the day when God judges the secrets of human hearts through Christ Jesus. So my gospel declares.[9]

St. Paul is declaring that whether we have *revelation* by the law and the gospel as Jews and Christians do in sacred Scriptures, or, like the Gentiles, we have only the revelation of nature, the word God is speaking through His creation, we are responsible for acknowledging Him as Elohim, for worshiping Him as Creator.

Such worship is our ultimate means of denying the old, false, usurping self-in-separation, and of the freeing of the true self into union with God. We become *makers* when we worship God as Elohim for, created in His image, His likeness within us is thus nourished and strengthened. To find one's true identity is to be open to one's true and highest vocation, for Elohim blesses the work of our hearts and hands when we function in His image.[10] Otherwise, when we worship the creature, the self, we are given over to all manner of *uncreative* and *destructive* behavior. We further mar and diminish the image of Elohim in us; we lose our identity as sons of God. We are no longer God-conscious, but self-conscious.

Another principal name for our God is *Yehovah*, and pictures Him in covenant relation with His creation. This Hebrew word is used over 6,400 times in Scripture. Our Creator God, Elohim, the Three-In-One, made provision for fallen man (all of us) to once again be linked with Him. This is the Good News, the gospel, the truth of Christ *in* us, healing us of our separation. It is the truth of the Incarnation and of the cross, the "new and living way opened for us through the curtain, that is, his [Christ's] body."[11]

The Old Covenant as well as the New is a gospel, a Good News, for as St. Paul reminds us: "This gospel God announced *beforehand* in sacred scriptures [Old Testament] through his prophets. It is about his Son. . . ."[12] The Old Covenant, by its blood sacrifices, foreshadowed the New (that is, Yehovah's covenant with us in and by the blood of His Son). And in a way past our understanding, the Father and the Son are one. The God of the Old Testament, Yehovah and Elohim, the God who is faithful and true, who is all loving-kindness, came into our world in the Son—gave Himself for our salvation. This is why the cross is right at the center of our faith. He who is love, peace, truth, righteousness, faithfulness gives Himself *for* us and *to* us. He lives in us. This is *glory*, fullness of *being*. This is identity. It is this we choose, or fail to choose. Fallen man endlessly attempts to find other ways to be healed, paths or methods that bypass the Incarnation and the cross. But in the end, we make one of two choices. We choose either the heaven of the realized identity in God, or the hell of the self-in-separation.

Obedience is the key. And to obey God is to listen to Him.

Six

Listening For the Healing Word

He sent his word to heal them and bring them alive out of the pit of death.–(Psalm 107:20, NEB)

Seeing the Invisible

Yesterday on entering a church for Sunday Eucharist, my eyes were drawn to the center where a baptismal font was readied. My eyes were instantly opened and I saw (for the briefest moment) the Lord standing there, bending over the waters. I immediately sensed the love and prayer that filled the sanctuary and I knew, even though I was a newcomer to the place, that Christ was wonderfully formed in the midst of a worshiping people here. During the baptismal liturgy, several people were surprised to find themselves weeping. They too were sensing the Presence of the Lord in a special way in our midst. There was a time in my life when I would have had difficulty containing my joy and channeling it aright after such a "seeing."[1] But not so now, for I know that He is with me, whether or not I apprehend Him in some unusual way.

Years ago when I first began to listen to God after having inquired of Him in prayer, He sent a word to my heart that has been a key in my own spiritual life and in my vocation as His disciple. I had been meditating upon Isaiah 58, and had asked the Lord about the *fast* that I should keep, most earnestly desiring that it be one acceptable unto Him. The following words I wrote as they were spoken to my heart, even though they seemed at first to have little to do with fasting:

> Keep Me with you all through the day. Do not delegate Me to a portion of your day. I created you, I died for you. Persevere with Me as I have persevered with you.

The word *persevere* struck the strings of my heart as no other word could, for only I knew the depths of God's faithfulness in persevering with me. And He was asking me to persevere with Him *as He had persevered with me*. Tears come to my eyes even now at such a word sent by the Spirit, one meant to reverberate in my heart and soul throughout my earthly pilgrimage.

That we might be more fully present to God is the very reason for fasting. By a physical fast we seek to quiet the demands of the body, thereby humbling it so that we *can* hear and be obedient to that word the Lord is speaking to us. It is then we can repent aright, and make the necessary prayers of intercession and atonement for others.

With the word *persevere*, I understood the spiritual discipline it would take to practice His Presence. We live in an age when it is particularly difficult to acknowledge the unseen. For the unbeliever as well as for the Christian who knows only an uncomprehending or even outright unbelieving church fellowship, "What is concrete but immaterial can be kept in view only by painful effort," as C. S. Lewis wrote. It is only too easy for Christians to think abstractly about God, His presence *with* them and *within* them, about angelic beings, and about what happens to themselves in Baptism and in Holy Communion when neither the angels nor the Holy Spirit are visible to their mortal eyes. To begin to "keep in view" the great Unseen Real (Transcendent and Immanent) is to begin to practice the Presence of God, and this is our single most important spiritual discipline. This was the fast to which God was calling me. I have not arrived, but am still persevering, and find that all my joy and any wholeness as well as ministry that I have is in this fast.

This, the knowledge that God is truly with us—that it is possible to be in familiar communion with Him—is the primary need of every lonely, suffering soul. Our "work" as ministers to those who suffer is that of praying, "Come, Lord Jesus,"[2] and then of inviting each and every soul into the healing Presence. This is, of course, apparent and should be standard for those who would minister in Christ's name; but it is perfectly amazing how many millions of words in "counseling" preempt and replace this one needful thing. This morning, prayerfully seeking guidance for this chapter, I was again reminded of this:

> Know that I AM *with* you, that I most truly do *indwell* you. This is the knowledge that all who sincerely seek my healing hunger for. This is experienced and made real as the minister invokes My Presence and invites needy ones to walk into Me. In Me they experience a love and faithfulness that is eternal—the substantive Love for which they have hungered.

In this way persons are not only healed, but come into union with God. They come to *know* Him. This *knowing* is not a "direct 'knowledge about' *(savoir)*" God, but a " 'knowledge-by-acquaintance' *(connaître)*," a " 'Tasting,' of Love Himself" that "the humblest of us, in a state of Grace," can know.[3]

In this kind of relationship we cease to look for signs or some sort of sensory proof of His Presence and begin rather to delight ourselves in Him. He is our goal. We practice His Presence with us as we read the Scriptures, as we pray, as we ride in our cars, as we move through our duties and our play. We do not reprimand ourselves if we forget, but rejoice in the remembering once again. In the doing of this, we find that He is often closest when our sensory being is the least aware. Just as the best time to pray is often when we least "feel" like it, so it is that He manifests Himself in such a way that our sensory being is alerted when we least expect this to happen. Thus we overcome the twentieth-century barriers to *belief*, and no longer stumble at the unseen.

Hearing the Inaudible

Knowing that Jesus is truly Emmanuel, God with us, and learning to practice His Presence is vital to being healed and remaining healed. This practice of the Presence is not a method, but a walk with a Person—and in this walk there is always healing. And there is also, as the Scriptures and our experience plainly shows, an ongoing dialogue. Listening to God then is a vital part of the practice of the Presence.

This listening is indispensable in the ministry of Christian healing. Henri Nouwen writes that it is "possible to experience the relationship between pastor and counselee as a way of entering together into the loving silence of God and waiting there for the healing Word."[4] This is the ministry I've been sharing about throughout this book. We are called to listen for the creative, healing Word, and to teach others so to do.

Listening to God through the Scriptures

"The sacred writings . . . have power to make you wise and lead you to salvation through faith in Christ Jesus," wrote the Apostle Paul to his beloved young protégé, Timothy.[5] We can never finish plumbing the depths of the treasures God has given us in the Sacred Writings. They are given by inspiration of God, and these, the *lectio divina* (sacred texts), are variously called the Word, the Word of God, the Word of Christ, the Word of Truth, as well as by other epithets such as the Book of the Lord, the Book of the Law, the Sword of the Spirit, the Oracles of God. The first principle in beginning to listen to God is that of taking the sacred texts into our very spirits and souls by prayerful meditation upon them. His word then "abides in us," burning as an inner light, and we cry out to God. This is *oratio*, responsive speech born of God's word aflame within.

The Sacred Writings support our spiritual life, and Jesus emphasizes this when He quotes Moses: "It is written: 'Man does not live on bread alone, but on every word that comes from the mouth of God.' "[6] The Scriptures give to us the standard of truth as well as the foundation and balance we must have:

> Fasten on the belt of truth; . . . let the shoes on your feet be the gospel of peace, to give you firm footing.[7]

Any other word coming to us, from whatever direction, is tried by the Scriptures. Paul and Silas successfully brought the message of Christ's death and resurrection to the Jews of Beroea because those people studied their Scriptures for proof of what these early Christian disciples were saying:

> They received the message with great eagerness, studying the scriptures every day to see whether it was as they said. Many of them therefore became believers, and so did a fair number of Gentiles, women of standing as well as men.[8]

The Scriptures have been called God's love letter to His people. In them He tells us what He is like—faithful and full of loving-kindness toward all who put their trust in Him. To meditate on God's Word is to meditate on His love for us—a love that in and with His Word floods "our inmost heart through the Holy Spirit he has given us."[9] To know that God loves *even me* is another desperate need of every suffering soul. As we meditate upon His love letter to us, making our wills one with His, we begin to grasp "what is the breadth and length and height and depth of the love of Christ, and to know it, though it is beyond knowledge."[10]

Listening Prayer

You shall know his power today if you will listen to his voice.[11]

The next step in prayer is exceedingly valuable to our spiritual growth, but it is the most neglected aspect of prayer in our day. It is the prayer of quiet listening for His voice, for His response to the cry of our hearts that has burst forth in speech toward Him. In this way our hearts remain open for the reception of His guidance, His exhortation, His word of wisdom or knowledge that comes in response to our cry. In learning to practice His Presence, we bring every thought of our minds, every imagination of our hearts into subjection to Christ who is Lord of our lives. In listening to Him, we exchange *our* way of seeing and doing for *His*.

Isaiah, prophesying of Christ the obedient Servant who was to come, said:

He will not judge by what he sees with his eyes, or decide by what he hears with his ears; but with righteousness he will judge the needy, with justice he will give decisions for the poor of the earth.[12]

And this is exactly what Jesus did: He judged by what He heard the Father speak; in the power of the Spirit, He did only what He saw the Father doing.[13]

We too, even as our Lord, listen in order to be the obedient disciple, in order to do the works of God:

For sword, take that which the Spirit gives you—the words that come from God.[14]

Listening to God is the most effective tool we have in our "healing kit," for by it we know how to collaborate with His Spirit. Teaching others to listen is one of the most valuable lessons we as spiritual directors can give them; by this freedom to hear, they pass from immaturity (being under the Law or laws) to maturity (the walk with Christ in the Spirit), both as persons and as Christians. The Lord Himself becomes their chief counselor and guide, and our vocation is made easier.

In granting space and time in our busy lives quietly to listen, we prepare and make more room in our minds and hearts to receive the word the Spirit sends throughout the day. Agnes Sanford once heard the Spirit tell her not to board a certain plane. She did not and the plane crashed. Later, when she told this story to a group, one woman rather angrily asked her why God would speak to her and not to others. Agnes immediately replied, "Oh, I think He was speaking to all of us. . . . But so few listen." We need to know what the Spirit is saying to us in the midst of our activities and emergencies, and that listening is learned by this step in prayer—that of taking time to listen and commune with God. We are called to teach people to pray. And perhaps that is why this step in prayer is so neglected. A trusted spiritual guide is usually needed to teach us so to pray, one in the fellowship of God's listening people whose spiritual gifts and understanding sharpens and completes ours.

Listening to God Is Vitally Important in the Process of Becoming Persons

> The prayer preceding all prayer is "May it be the real I who speaks. May it be the real Thou that I speak to."[15]

The fallen self cannot know itself. As we have seen, we do not know who we are and will search for our identity in someone or something other than God until we find ourselves in Him. And it is only in Him that we become persons. In the Presence, conversing with Him, we find that the "old man"—the sinful, the neurotic, the sickly compulsive, the seedy old actor within—is not *the Real*, but that these are simply the false selves that can never be rooted in God. We find that God is the Real and that He calls the real "I" forward, separating us from our sicknesses and sins. We then no longer define ourselves by our sins, neuroses, and deprivations, but by Him whose healing life cleanses and indwells us. From being bent toward the creature—the horizontal position of the Fall—we straighten up into the completing union with the Creator—the vertical, listening position of the free creature. We find that we are in Him and that He is in us. Thus in the Presence, listening to the word the Spirit sends, spiritual and psychological healing takes place. Our Lord sends a word—of joy, judgment, instruction, guidance. And that word, if hidden away in an obedient heart, will work toward the integration of that personality. As I listen and obey, I *become*.

Throughout a series of talks given to clergy by Fr. Alan Jones, he repeated these words: "We either contemplate or we exploit." He further stated:

Only in silence comes the Word—It is then we discern the pattern of the Spirit. It is then we are available to our deepest self as it unfolds in the Spirit.

"We either contemplate or we exploit." We either learn to listen to God or we manipulate. We manipulate others and we ourselves are even gladly manipulated in order to alleviate the loneliness of our separation from the voice of God. In the Presence, listening, I unmask, I take off my many false faces and my true self comes face to face with Jesus. If I look for me, I will never find me—only my many fragmented selves. But if I look for Him, I will eventually find that the whole of me is united in Jesus.

In true prayer, I face all the facts. I begin to tell the true story, the true tale of my life:

Thou dost lay bare our iniquities before thee, and our lusts in the full light of thy Presence.[16]

In this light, the true facts of my existence, no matter how monstrous or how petty, are brought into conversation with God.

"The depressed or afflicted person," says Dr. Frank Lake, "has stopped praying because he cannot, or feels he cannot, turn either the depravities of rage and lust, or the deprivations of faithlessness, anxiety, and emptiness, into prayer."[17] In bringing needy ones into the Presence where we listen to God together, this is exactly what we help them do. Once "prayer as communication with God" is "reestablished . . . he can bring his complaints, objections, demands, accusations, resentments, doubts, and disbeliefs out of hiding, and into conversation with the pastor and with God."[18] My compulsions, addictions, anxieties, unreasonable fears—all these are acknowledged and brought into the conversation with God; and as I listen, He sends the word that breaks the pattern of immaturity, the bondage of sin. I struggle free from these patterns, and from erroneous ways of perceiving myself.

Furthermore, and as important in my becoming the *maker* God created me to be, I find that along with the dark things I have feared to face heretofore come up bright and beautiful things as well:

> Radiant things, delights and inspirations, come to the surface as well as snarling resentments and nagging lusts.[19]

These too I had feared to acknowledge.

Desire, in my opinion, is among the most important of these "radiant things" that must be allowed to surface. When the true self is cowering under layers of veils and self-consciousness, it fears both the selfishness (carnality) from which it is not yet free, and the disappointment of its deepest hopes and aspirations were they ever allowed to come to the light. When He alone is our goal, our eye becomes single,[20] and we gain what some of our Fathers called the virtue of disinterestedness. In seeking only Him who is our righteousness we begin to see more clearly, and purity of heart and life ensues. *Sanctity* (rather than "happiness," "love," "material gain," and so on) is then our correlative aim; it is the flipside of our prime goal. We can therefore safely desire even those things we've been so fearful to acknowledge before, because they are wholly offered to Him. Listening prayer is holy converse; it is holy interaction with God. He assures us, and we know most certainly, that He will remove the chaff from the wheat, that He will transmute the desire when and where necessary, that He will elevate it to higher planes when our perception of His will for us is too low.

The following is Fr. John Gaynor Banks's meditation on desire, one inspired by this line from the poet Traherne: "Desire like a God that you may be satisfied like a God."

> MASTER: Desire is a mighty force, one of your most divine attributes! Whatsoever things ye *desire* when ye pray, *believe* that ye have received them and ye shall have them! See the Godlike quality of desire. For it is part of the Atomic energy of the soul. The Kingdom of Heaven within you is operated through desire. Do not quench it or crush it or suppress it. Rather *offer* it to Me. Offer Me your most elementary desires, your craving for happiness, for love, for self-expression, for well-being, for success, for joy, on any level of your being—offer these desires freely and without shame to Me and I will transmute them so that you shall achieve release and fulfillment and complete freedom from frustration.[21]

I have seen many a depressed person's healing begin as we quieten ourselves in His Presence and ask Him to bring up the deepest desire of the heart, that one the sufferer has been too fearful ever to acknowledge before. Then conversation with God about it begins. It takes the real self to truly desire, and in its desiring all that is good, beautiful, and true, it more quickly and wonderfully functions in the image of its Maker.

In listening prayer we gain the hallowed space and time needed to befriend our emotions, those jaded or stunted in the past, or those feared and rejected and therefore repressed. Our emotions of anger, grief, joy, love, and shame, along with the deeply repressed desires of our hearts, are brought into this holy converse with God. In His loving acceptance, our emotional being grows into a delicate and gentle balance with our sensory and intellectual being. We need no longer be shaped by our emotional needs and deprivations, but rather will see them healed.

In this converse with God, for the moment we have opened as widely as we can our hearts to the Lord. He has known all along what was there and what was needed. Now our *wills* are one with His, and we have consented to yield up to Him what has heretofore been carefully garnered in our hearts. We are now ready for that most important moment in prayer. True prayer is, like all else that partakes of the *Real*, incarnational; that is, it is a reception of God's life. We ask Him to come in more fully, and to fill all the spaces of our being (especially those we have just emptied) with Himself. This is the moment for

> letting that other larger, stronger, quieter life come flowing in. . . . We can do it only for moments at first. But from those moments the new sort of life will be spreading through our systems because now we are letting Him work at the right part of us.[22]

Few of us learn to listen to God for the healing Word without being brought to the end of ourselves in some tragic way or another. Aleksandr Solzhenitsyn, who was later to write, "One word of truth outweighs the world," first became present to that Word and to himself in the horrors of a Communist prison camp. There in that unspeakable place he first found the time and inclination to listen to his own heart and to God. Himself a Communist, he was weighed down by the lies of the world, the flesh and the devil in general, and of the Communist world in particular. As he learned to listen, the *real* Aleksandr Solzhenitsyn came forward, an event the rest of us have reason to be grateful for, because he is one who listens well to the word of truth and witnesses powerfully to the whole world of what he hears. In that enforced suffering and loneliness, he was raised above the mind-set of the age and therefore could (amazingly enough) cry out, "Bless you, prison, for having been in my life!"

"Know thyself!" There is nothing that so aids and assists the awakening of Omniscience within us as insistent thoughts about one's own transgressions, errors, mistakes. . . . And that is why I turn back to the years of my imprisonment and say, . . . "Bless you, prison." . . . I nourished my soul there. "Bless you, prison, for having been in my life!"[23]

He is now one of the few great prophets calling out to a blinded and deafened world, struggling in its own network of lies.

In listening prayer we remain keenly aware not only of our prime identity, that of child of God, but also of our secondary identity, that of sinner. In the Presence we recognize the false selves and allow them to fall from us as old cloaks or hardened shells. We no longer have to practice their presence. St. Paul says it this way:

There is no necessity for us to obey our unspiritual selves or to live unspiritual lives.[24]

Our lower nature has no claim upon us; we are not obliged to live on that level. If you do so, you must die. But if by the Spirit you put to death all the base pursuits of the body, then you will live.[25]

The true self, thereby continuing to recognize its secondary identity as sinner, remains free to move always from that center within where Christ dwells—that is, out of its prime identity. This self realizes that being a Christian can, if it doesn't make one a great deal better, make one a great deal worse:

For the Supernatural, entering a human soul, opens to it new possibilities both of good and evil. From that point the road branches: one way to sanctity, humility, the other to spiritual pride, self-righteousness, persecuting zeal. And no way back to the mere humdrum virtues of the unawakened soul.[26]

Solzhenitsyn, suffering with abdominal cancer and lying on rotting straw in his prison's hospital ward, discovered these two identities, this brokenness within all men:

> Gradually it was disclosed to me that the line separating good and evil passes not through states, not between classes, not between political parties either—but right through every human heart—and through all human hearts. This line shifts. Inside us, it oscillates with the years. And even within hearts overwhelmed with evil, one small bridgehead of good is retained. And even in the best of all hearts there remains . . . an unuprooted small corner of evil. [27]

As I wrote in an earlier book,

> Pride is the great sin, the one which leads to every other vice, and it can crop up in the redeemed with far more disastrous results than in the unregenerate. The unregenerate self is one that wills to be separate, to be autonomous, to put itself first. The same free will that makes such an evil possible in the first place can, at any stage of the spiritual life, cease to choose the good and again choose itself. John, in Pilgrim's Regress, [28] finds himself dying many deaths, and learns that this dying is the only escape from Death. Our escape from Death consists largely in our learning to die daily to the "old man" and in regular acts of repentance followed by receptions of God's forgiveness. [29]

And it is only in listening prayer that we know our own hearts, and therefore what to confess.

Conflict and struggle are important elements in our metamorphosis as persons. We must learn as ministers never to interrupt, through misplaced sympathy or empathy, the painful process whereby a soul is being raised from its stupor and deadness. This is most often done in Christian circles by encouraging the person to "bend" toward ourselves. But we can never take another's loneliness away. Henri Nouwen speaks powerfully to this current delusion:

There is much mental suffering in our world. But some of it is suffering for the wrong reason because it is born out of the false expectation that we are called to take each other's loneliness away. When our loneliness drives us away from ourselves into the arms of our companions in life, we are, in fact, driving ourselves into excruciating relationships, tiring friendships and suffocating embraces.[30]

Our pastoral task is to help every needy one face his inner loneliness, and there begin to hear God and his own true self. Every one of us, not just the ones who are the most visibly wounded by the darkness in man and in the world, has to face the inner loneliness and separation from God and then begin the rigorous but sternly magnificent work of converting the "desert of loneliness"[31] within into the spaciously beautiful "garden of solitude"[32] where the true self comes forward. This is the self capable of friendship, capable of Christian fellowship. Its identity is no longer in the creature.

In view of the struggle set for all men, we as ministers must not faint or even be overly dismayed when one we have seen come so far has what seems to us an almost irreparable lapse or fall back into the old self and its ways. The butterfly moth provides a wonderful picture of the struggle that each soul must go through in its becoming. It is painful to see the moth struggle inside its cocoon in its effort to emerge. But if we take scissors and snip off the top of the cocoon, the moth will never fly. It is in the struggle against its outer shell or self that its wings develop and become strong. Then, from a lowly worm, gorging itself all day and dragging its tummy on a tree limb, at length it metamorphoses into a gorgeous creature that flies, its wings bearing the colors and designs of an omnipotent hand. There are times before it emerges that its struggle ceases for a while, and we wonder if it has given up its painful work, or even if it has died within its woven shell. So it is at times with those for whom we pray.

In the case of those who are being healed of serious sexual neuroses, ministers can quickly panic or be discouraged when the person falls back momentarily into old patterns and defense mechanisms. But as they listen to God for the sufferer who seeks help, they will receive that word of wisdom, of knowledge, of exhortation, etc. that is needed to help the person once again to seek the Presence of God, to listen to Him, and to get on in his *becoming*. He has simply for the moment ceased to struggle into the vertical, listening, free position, and has bent back toward the creature.

Those, for instance, who are freed from severe lesbian or homosexual neuroses, but are still in the process of accepting themselves, can be swiftly and powerfully overtaken by the "cannibal" compulsion (see Chapter 3). This is an exceedingly strong projection of the part of themselves they cannot acknowledge onto another of their own sex. Without pastoral help these persons do not recognize what is happening, just as they cannot as yet acknowledge and accept the unaffirmed and unintegrated attributes of their own personalities.

One young girl, her healing nothing short of miraculous, is a case in point. While still in the process of accepting herself and of learning how to relate meaningfully to others, she came into close contact with a woman who mirrored her yet unaffirmed attributes. In fact, the woman *was very like she herself would be* when she was fully functioning in her God-given vocation. Failing to recognize the projection mechanism in her immediate attraction to the woman, her "love" first took the form of a helping hand, then a protective arm, then a devouring mother-love. It ended in a *deliberate* and in her words *angrily rebellious* reopening of her mind to the old lesbian compulsion, a predictable conclusion to the unchecked projection. Her fall was traumatic and one she immediately repented of with all her heart. But it was also tragic in terms of the loss of the woman's friendship and of other friends as well as her professional position, all of which meant much to her and reflected her great strides up and out of mental and emotional darkness. Although she lost much that was dear to her, she is wiser now. And she has gained new and even stronger wings with which to fly.

Also, those who are freed from lesbian or homosexual neuroses, but are still in the process of being healed of separation-anxiety or of other severe deprivational neuroses, can be powerfully overtaken by the need for another's arms around them. They may say something like the young man said who wrote me, "I did not want anything 'hard-core.' I just wanted to be held, I wanted someone's arms tight around me." The need here is not for another man's arms, but for the gift of well-being, something he never gained in his mother's arms. To be held and kissed by another man will only add to his symbolic confusion. Even he, still hurting, realizes this and said of such an experience: "It was a weird half-father, half-lover kind of attempt that I wonder about." And he does well both to wonder about and to turn from this dangerous kind of solace which will keep him from continuing to face the inner loneliness and from inviting God into the midst of it. His love, flooding into that chasm of dread and deprivation, will complete the healing needed. But obedience (the vertical position) is imperative. Only then is God permitted to do the work needed.

I know how frightening and guilt-laden the word *obedience* can be to the homosexual sufferer, the one who has long suffered mental and emotional pain (has literally hated himself) as he struggled endlessly and without reward, losing battle after battle against his strange inner tendencies and compulsions, and against temptations as repulsive and frightening to himself as to anyone else. He has often prayed, and prayed, and prayed, and yet he is tormented, unchanged.

For this very reason, many who pray for such sufferers have not emphasized the fact that homosexual activity is sinful, but have rather emphasized it as the psychological sickness that it also usually is. Now, however, since many seek to justify homosexual activity, we need to stress the fact that it is sinful, and that obedience to God's revealed will is indeed a happy thing. Only in this obedience can the sufferer be freed from this diseased form of love.

The prophet Isaiah cries out to God, "For You have hid your face from us and have delivered us into the (consuming) power of our iniquities."[33] For pastors and counselors within Christendom to accept and condone homosexuality rather than to heal it is to deliver the individual into the consuming power of his own sin and sickness. Furthermore, it is to become party to it.

We are the Household of Faith only as we are in obedience to Christ. This is not a gospel of works, but a gospel of love. He who loves Christ, as the Scriptures plainly teach, *obeys* Him. The hands of the healing Christ are tied to the very extent that we choose not to dwell in Him, but rather to dwell in quite another spirit, that of disobedience and rebellion. Rebellion spawns all kinds of confusion.

There is no room for the divided mind here. We either obey God in this matter or we are given over to a reprobate mind. We know that God has declared homosexual activity to be iniquitous and therefore damning to the soul. As pastors and counselors, we must help that soul turn from the very thing that is killing it. To teach obedience is the loving thing to do.

Listening Prayer Is Vitally Connected to the True Imagination

The truly imaginative experience is an intuition of the *Real*. At its highest level, it is the experience of receiving from God, whether by word, vision or (greatest of all) an incarnation or infilling of the Holy Spirit. The faculty within man which apprehends the Real—that is, acknowledges the Presence and worshipfully listens in creaturely awe and obedience—is the intuitive organ the Bible calls the heart.

The Picture-making Faculty of the Heart Is Not Itself the True or Higher Imagination

We must stress the fact that the picture-making faculty of the heart is not itself the true or higher imagination. Pictures are the language of the heart and like icons are merely images through which the Real is to shine. If the image is mistaken for the Real, it becomes "self-conscious" and so a "dumb idol." The heart's capacity to symbolically image what it intuits is to be differentiated from the intuition itself.

When an angel of the Lord appeared to Joseph in a dream and said, "Joseph, son of David, do not be afraid to take Mary home with you as your wife. It is by the Holy Spirit that she has conceived this child," Joseph's heart intuited both the presence of the angel and the angel's message aright. Had he attempted to literalize what he saw by saying, "All angels look like the one who appeared in my dream," he would have mistaken the conscious mind's way of seeing for that of the heart's. He may even have lost the true message in an attempt to make it analytically logical. When the angel Gabriel was sent to Mary, he went into the town of Nazareth and into Mary's presence and said, "Greetings, most favored one! The Lord is with you." She intuited Gabriel's presence and message aright. How her heart pictured the unseen was yet another matter.

The heart's capacity to see that which is true and real though invisible to the physical eye is not well understood in a day when the conscious and analytical ways of knowing are valued to the exclusion of the other. Both ways of knowing are important and complementary one to the other. Both are vitally important to belief, art, and the good of reason.[34]

To most of us the word imagination is a vague one.

> The dictionary defines it as "the action . . . of forming a mental image or concept of what is not present to the senses." Another definition denotes the imaginative faculty

itself by which these images or concepts are formed. A third refers to the "power which the mind has of forming concepts beyond those derived from external objects (the 'productive imagination')." This power refers not only to fancy but, more important, to creative or poetic genius, "the power of framing new and striking intellectual conceptions."[35]

This last definition, in its reference to creative or poetic genius, approaches our definition of the true or higher imagination. This is the level of poetic awe and is, as we shall see, closely related to religious awe:

> There are several levels even to the truly imaginative, and we must differentiate between that which begins in merely poetic awe and that which includes religious awe. Similarly, we intuit the Real in at least three kinds—the realms of Nature, Super-nature, and the Real Presence of God. The awe differs as the *kinds* of reality to be intuited differ, though Absolute Reality, in the Person of the Holy Spirit, can find His way through any one of the three.
>
> It is in the Object, that which invokes the awe, that the difference lies. "The form of the desired is in the desire." (C. S. Lewis, *Surprised by Joy*, p. 220) When the heavens were opened "in the thirtieth year, in the fourth month, on the fifth day of the month" and the prophet Ezekiel saw "visions of God" he fell upon his face in worshipful awe. In the midst of this he heard a Voice speaking: "And when he spoke to me, the Spirit entered into me and set me upon my feet." Ezekiel was then indwelt by the Object. This is religious awe, and the Object that inspired it was God.
>
> In poetic awe the artist sees, with his newborn intuition, one blade of grass or one dewdrop as it really is. His experience differs from Ezekiel's in that the object giving rise to the awe differs. But the parallels are definitely there. Looking to the object, the artist forgets himself, and in loving that which he sees he becomes totally "absorbed" in it. Possessed by the creative idea, he feels compelled to transpose it into material form. This is poetic awe, capable at any moment of becoming not less, but more, than poetic awe.

It is often with a profound sense of transfigured awe that the artist or the mystic perceives the truths of super-nature or, on a higher level, of God. Then, sometimes flat on his face over what he feels to be his utter inadequacy, he attempts to pass the vision on. Always, too, there is the gap between that which is seen and heard and that which is finally captured—on canvas, in stone, in poetry, in melody. To one who is not an artist or a mystic it seems incredible that Michelangelo felt himself to be a fumbler, and that Isaiah, when he saw the Lord sitting high and lifted up, felt himself to be lost and a man of unclean lips. Even so, it is in humility and awe, and with a plea for incarnation, a plea for enablement to be a servant to the work, that the

artist, the priest or mystic, sees the Real, and desires to capture at least a gleam of it in his art or in his ministry, in the work of his hands and sacramentally, as it were, through the blessing of his hands. Hereby the transcendent and the eternal shines through the lowly and the finite. We see that there is within

> the mountains, stars and seas, the eternal splendor, rhythm, and melody inherent in the very fabric of the universe; within the individual person, a universe enclosed in human form; within the communion cup, the living body and blood of Christ.[36]

Thus we see that an intuition of the Real Presence differs only in degree from the sudden intuition of a truth in Nature or even in Super-nature (i.e., the numinous awe one would experience in the presence of an angel or any created supernatural being).[37]

> But the manner in which the revelation comes and the intuitive and experiential nature of the *knowing* is much the same.[38]

Seeing the Unseen with the Eyes of the Heart

Our sole avenue to reality, as C. S. Lewis has said, is through prayer, sacrament, repentance, and adoration[39]—that is, through the deep heart's way of knowing. There has been much said throughout this book about seeing with the eyes of the heart as an important part of this *knowing*, and as an important part of prayer.

Oswald Chambers understands the heart's need to fix its eyes on God, and the interchange that begins between God and man when this happens. Commenting on Isaiah 26:3 (R.V., margin), "Thou wilt keep him in perfect peace whose imagination is stayed on Thee," Chambers says:

> Is your imagination stayed on God or is it starved? The starvation of the imagination is one of the most fruitful sources of exhaustion and sapping in a worker's life. If you have never used your imagination to put yourself before God, begin to do it now. It is no use waiting for God to come; you must put your imagination away from the face of idols and look unto Him and be saved. Imagination is the greatest gift God has given us and it ought to be devoted entirely to Him. If you have been bringing every thought into captivity to the obedience of Christ, it will be one of the greatest assets to faith when the time of trial comes, because your faith and the Spirit of God will work together.[40]

Commenting on Isaiah 40:26, "Lift up your eyes on high, and behold who hath created these things," Chambers says,

> The people of God in Isaiah's day had starved their imagination by looking on the face of idols, and Isaiah made them look up at the heavens, that is, he made them begin to use their imagination aright. . . .
> The test of spiritual concentration is bringing the imagination into captivity. Is your imagination looking on the face of an idol? Is the idol yourself? Your work? . . . If your imagination is starved, do not look back to your own experience; it is God Whom you need. Go right out of yourself, away from the face of your idols, away from everything that has been starving your imagination. Rouse yourself, take the gibe that

Isaiah gave the people, and deliberately turn your imagination to God.

One of the reasons of stultification in prayer is that there is no imagination, no power of putting ourselves deliberately before God. . . . Imagination is the power God gives a saint to posit himself out of himself into relationships he never was in.[41]

Chambers's insight into the heart's way of seeing and knowing is profound and true. That is why he is one of the great devotional writers of this century.

Listening to God Is Vitally Related to the Gifts of the Holy Spirit

Prayer for psychological healing (as well as healing of the spirit and body of man) can only be understood in relation to the *"spirituals,"* that term we translate from the Greek as *"gifts"* of the Holy Spirit. To minister in this kind of prayer is to move in one or another of the healing gifts of the Spirit. When we do this in Jesus' name, and *as we listen,* He sends us that "word of knowledge," that "word of wisdom," that supernatural faith, and so on that is needed to see the person cleansed and healed.

These *spirituals*[42] as well as all the *fruits*[43] of the Spirit, reside in God and have to do with His Presence with us and within us. There is Another who lives in me. He has the Spirit without measure. With Him are all the gifts and all the fruits of the Holy Spirit. Because Jesus, *the Gift,* lives in me, the gifts and the fruits of His life are present and can radiate through me. I am thus empowered by His indwelling Presence to heal in His name. We bring others into His Presence, and see them healed. We then teach them to practice His Presence, that is to "see" with the eyes of their hearts, to "hear" with the ears of their hearts the One who is with them, the Word who has never yet stopped speaking to the creatures He loves and calls His very own children. So we teach them to listen and to walk with their

Creator and Savior so that their healing may continue, and so they too may become channels of His life to another.

We bring them into what has been most wondrously called the Great Dance.[44] It is the divine dance of healed relationships. Let us imagine the Great Dance for a moment. It is love flowing down from the uncreated into the created, and from thence into all other created beings. To continue to receive of the "bright metal"[45] being poured into it, each creature must become a channel of this love to others, for it is in the nature of love that it must flow. And it is by virtue of love flowing through him that man begins to bless and to name his fellows, calling forth the real "I," and that he begins to bless and name the beasts, the plants, and even the inanimate creation. If we allow our imaginations the freedom, we can "see" each person, wholly giving himself in perfect obedience to the divine rhythm flowing through the dancers, clasping hands with the person on his right and the one on his left, until all men are hand in hand. We then see that they are somehow encircling all creation, and that all creation is being "taken into" them.[46] The "rhythm" flowing through them is divine energy, and our final image is of all creation on tiptoe with *joy*.

Appendix:
Listening to Our Dreams

The person suffering from a homosexual identity crisis is invariably separated from a valid part of his own being. Dreams, once we learn to read their symbolic messages, can help us recognize that part from which we are estranged. In order to demonstrate that prayer for the healing of the homosexual identity crisis is not that much different from prayer for the removal of any other psychological block, I would like to tell a part of my own personal story as I related it to Matthew. As in Matthew's case (see Chapter 3), God used dreams to show me the part of myself I could not acknowledge.

Matthew was at first overwhelmed by what his recurring homosexual dream *really meant:* that he was looking at the other admirable young man and in fact loving a lost part of himself, a part that he could not recognize and accept. And it seemed almost too good to be true that through prayer Christ would bring him into relationship with that lost part of himself. This was, after all, his first occasion to consider the symbolic language of the dream, as well as the first time he'd been challenged to believe there might be more to himself than he'd yet perceived or accepted. How all this could be I was only too happy to illustrate, and I did so with a story from my own life.

Such a healing prayer as this I could enter into with the greatest of enthusiasm and faith, for God had healed me of a writer's block—one that as in Matthew's case dissolved only after illumination was received from a healing of memories and a set of dreams. This block involved, to my amazement, being separated from the part of me that could or would write a book for publication.

The book was certainly within me, so to speak, and demanded to be put into writing. Madeleine L'Engle, author of many fine books, expresses such a thing this way: "A book comes up, takes hold of my skirt and won't let go until I've written it." C. S. Lewis's remark that he was "pregnant with book" is wonderfully meaningful to anyone who has within himself a book, poem, painting, or whatever, and has at the same time an agonizing block to the proper expression of it. Even worse for me was the sure conviction that the Lord had asked this of me, and was waiting for me to do it. For the longest time, therefore, I would pray, "Lord, how can I do this? I'm far too busy and I don't know what I could leave off doing." But no assurance would come that this was a valid excuse—just the gentle and unsettling knowledge that He was waiting for me to do it!

I certainly was busy—teaching two sections of Freshman English, working on a graduate degree, and conducting healing missions—not to mention a heavy involvement in the Church at the local level. Anyone involved in the healing ministry stays busy at home and abroad. My apologies and excuses for not getting the book written had every rationale, or so it seemed. But gradually, as I continued to ask friends to "please pray for me that I might obey the Lord and get this thing done," I began to realize that I had a psychological block—that something beyond what I could consciously understand was barring me from writing this book which was full-blown within me and crying for expression. I, like Matthew, could not recognize a part of me from which I was painfully estranged, and needed prayer for enablement *to accept that part of me who is a writer*, a part of "who I am," vital to fulfilling the work God has given my hands to do.

"I will bless the Lord who has given me counsel: in the night-time wisdom comes to me in my inward parts."[1] So declares David, Israel's shepherd king, and he could well be speaking of dreams here. That is how I would describe a series of six dreams that brought me face to face with the writer in me. In these dreams, she came right up out of the depths of my deep mind and presented herself to my astonished conscious attention. She first appeared as a feminine figure *unprepared*, but contemplating a leap over a swollen stream where a bridge *had once been*, but was long ago washed away. Against all odds, she jumped and was gravely, perhaps even fatally, injured in the leap. This dream and another revealed the childhood injury in which the block was rooted.

In another, she appeared as a figure *prepared* to cross a dangerous river, but fearful of exposure. In another, she appeared as an acrobatic dancer skilled, yet fearful of exposure. And finally, she appeared as an acrobatic high wire artist, performing with skill and precision, *exposed but no longer minding exposure*. Dreams are terribly frank, and my fear of exposure was symbolized by being scantily clothed—something not un-usual in the acrobatic dance or in highwire artistry. With the last figure, the writer (who necessarily exposes herself) and I came together. This understanding, along with prayer, brought quite an incredible healing.

The dreams, so briefly alluded to above, revealed that the *fear of exposure* was rooted in the consequences my family had suf-fered through the loss of my father. Please note that it was the consequences, and not the loss itself, for as I will share a little further on, I had already been healed of my grievous reaction to his sudden death: that of a deep sense of personal rejection by him. He died when I had just turned three, leaving my mother, myself, and my eighteen-month-old sister exposed, and for a time quite thrown out upon the world and others for the shelter we needed.

In the first dream the bridge over the stream of life was washed out, and the girl injured in trying to leap across. My father had been that bridge, and the flood of death had taken him away. That I had experienced his death as a personal rejection was totally lost to my conscious mind, both as a child and then for many of my adult years. This was so even though throughout my childhood and adult life I had had the recurring dream of searching for my father, of finding his casket, of hoping against hope that he might be alive. But this loss of my father formed no part of these six dreams. Rather, they consistently revealed the fear of exposure along with the concomitant deep feelings of inadequacy and inferiority as the direct consequence of being fatherless. And the little girl within me who felt all this was inextricably combined with the writer within.

Unlike Matthew, I was not projecting a part of me onto someone else and irrationally loving myself in that person. But I was, like him, successfully denying a valid part of myself—the part of me that had grievously reacted to my father's death, and the resulting loss of the love and security only he could bring to my mother, my little sister, and myself. In attempts to overcome the loss, I, like any good stoic, simply *denied* it. I steadfastly and consistently denied throughout my life the little girl in me who would *admit* her fear of rejection and exposure, inadequacy and inferiority, in the absence of a father. She it was who attempted to leap over the swollen river, rather than admit the missing bridge made it impossible.

I therefore had to confess *pride*. For feelings of inadequacy and inferiority (like those of presumption and superiority), no matter from what psychological injury they stem, are in the final analysis rooted in that sin. An important part of both Matthew's and Lisa's healing had to do with this same acknowledgment of the sin of pride. I believe that behind every writer's block,[2] indeed, at the bottom of every need for psychological healing, one will find the need to confess, "Lord, there is a part of me that has never confessed its need and pride, and therefore that part of me is still trying to be adequate apart from You, is still fearful and unable to wholly depend upon You." When my dreams revealed this condition in me, it would have been easy to go on denying these fears (as I had successfully done all my life) rather than to confess them to God.[3] In fact, *if I had not written the insights down immediately, they would have slipped back into the unconscious and have been just as lost to me as if they had never surfaced to consciousness.*

The confession of sin and reception of its absolution is the key to inner healing, and for this reason there is no power to heal the soul like that found in the power that Christ gives. This healing flows to the deepest levels of awareness, and the healing of those memories reveals the truest and deepest roots of our problems in relating to others and to ourselves. Thus I was healed of the writer's block, and completed soon thereafter my first book for publication.

The Projection Mechanism

Every rejection we are not healed of, we will project onto another. It is obvious then that we are at times the object of these projections as well as the perpetrator of them. In either case, these mechanisms are quickly revealed in prayers for inner healing. Matthew needed more understanding of this; so I went on to explain how it had worked in my case.

The projection mechanism was perhaps[4] at work in me—not, as in Matthew's case, a projection of the parts of myself I could not accept onto another, but as a projection of the overall rejection I had experienced in the loss of my father. It is probable that, as a child, this unconscious trauma found a conscious outlet in my feelings about the grandmother who came to live with us at the time of my father's death. If I had gone in search of the causes behind the writer's block and had arrived at merely what my conscious rational understanding could reveal through an analysis of the early events of my life, I would have said, "It was *all* Grandmother's fault. She never really liked me, and she surely never affirmed me in my bent toward writing, music and studies." But this, though one part true, would have been mostly false.

My grandmother, a fine old Southern country woman, was Scots by bloodline, and of the variety that was all practicality and brooked "no nonsense." My attempts to convert life into some understandable art form were often as not deemed by her both as a "putting on of airs" and—even more hurtful insofar as I was concerned—as a way of trying to outdo my younger sister, whom she greatly favored. My sister, full of fun and mischief, and not at all aware that there were such things as death and trouble to be contended with in the adult world, was a child my grandmother could love and understand.

Though thoroughly unconscious of the denial at work in my own life where my father was concerned, I had from earliest childhood been painfully aware of the consequences of his death as it affected my hard-working and fragile little mother. Born weighing less than three pounds, she had had a very precarious start in life and had never been physically strong. The chief fear of my early years was that she too would die. Though she more than made up for physical weakness in moral and spiritual strength and did not need my protection, I ran interference for her in every possible way my young mind could devise. I "mothered" my mother and was quick to sense any danger or hardship coming her way. Such a child as this, then, serious beyond her years, with a vivid memory of her father's death and aware of her mother's suffering, one who would try to understand life by interaction with the adult world at a very early age and *as a writer* later on, was the one always at variance with Grandma. That part of me was not affirmed.

Before the advent of the writer's block, I had experienced the healing of the deeper, underlying rejection caused by my reaction to my father's death. It happened at the first School of Pastoral Care (founded by Agnes Sanford and her husband, the Rev. Edgar Sanford) I attended. The group gathered there consisted of ministers, religious (nuns, teachers, monks, deacons), and various professionals in the medical, health, and educational fields, all of whom were involved in prayer for healing of the sick. I was deeply involved in the healing ministry, and had found the wholeness and meaning that only a fully committed and joyful relationship to Christ can bring. Through confession of every known sin in every period of my life, through reparation of it where needed and possible, through a wholehearted and free reception of God's incredible forgiving grace, and through prayerful waiting upon the Lord, I had received the healing of every known hurt and even disappointment!

But, as I was unaware of the psychological injury (rejection in this case) that had underlain much of my need for healing in the first place, I ended as amazed by what happened to me in a prayer for healing of memories as Matthew had been over the concept of why cannibals are cannibals. Even more important insofar as the healing ministry is concerned, the Lord proved to me beyond all shadow of doubt the validity of prayer for psychological healing—that He not only can, but delights in pointing out and bringing up the root traumas, no matter at what age in our lives they are experienced. And furthermore, it is not something *we* do; rather, it is what we allow *Him* to do!

Barbara Shlemon, a gifted leader in the ministry of healing, was praying this particular prayer, and she formed it chronologically, beginning in the present and going back toward birth and conception. When she got down to between age three and eighteen months, up popped the clearest voice imaginable from my deep heart: "Forgive your father for dying!" How ridiculous, I thought, to forgive one's father for dying. But I did it just the same. The clarion quality of that command to me is something never to be forgotten, much less doubted or denied. The fact that children take the loss of parents, however it comes about, as personal rejection was the subject of Barbara's sharing with us on the following day—the very thing God had so clearly shown me.

Several years later, as I faced the problem of the writer's block, my dreams revealed it to be rooted, not in this root rejection that had been revealed and healed, but in its consequences (fear of exposure) which had never been *admitted*. The whole matter of how I had as a child viewed my grandmother, though not a part of the dreams at all, was a consideration that grew out of these two healings. It followed then that I had to ask myself these questions: (1) How much of the unconscious rejection due to my father's death had I projected off onto my grandmother? (2) Was she unable to show me love and affection because I resented her as having replaced my father? (3) Unhealed rejections render us to varying extents unable to love. Had I been unable to love her and therefore been the cause of the break between us? I had to confess my sin of rejecting her.

Breaks in family relationships are tragic, and a tragedy for both of us, I think, was the fact that we never quite worked out our relationship in this life. With this understanding and my confession, however, as so often happens in healing of memories, what we failed to find in her lifetime was achieved after her death. We are now in a right relationship, for I find that I truly love my unreflective though well-meaning little Scots grandmother. I know this is so on several counts, but the most irrefutable one is, I suppose, that she who is now in the greater Presence of the Lord is certainly healed; and now that I am also, there is nothing but love between us.

Blocks to understanding the true tale of our lives,[5] and our need for confession and absolution are truly just that—blocks. Just as blind prejudice is truly unseeing, so are blocks, such as Matthew and I had, truly barriers. We could not master them by conscious effort and simply go around or leap over them. These blocks to our *becoming,* and to our usefulness in the Kingdom of God, point up the Church's need to recover the knowledge of how to pray effectively for their removal—in other words, our need to learn how to pray effectively for psychological healing. The wholeness and resulting maturity and freedom of the essential self or spirit is dependent in large part upon a person's achievement of psychological wholeness. Indeed, our spiritual wholeness is interwoven with the psychological, for we cannot fully confess our sins of pride and unlove until we are enabled to recognize them.

There is of course great healing virtue in the confession of those sins of which we are unaware: "Who can discern his lapses and errors? Clear me from hidden [and unconscious] faults."[6] But the fullest healing comes as we are able to face the hidden thing, confess it specifically, and yield it up to God. His forgiving and healing light then floods into that part of us which is in darkness, and our sins are dispersed "like a dissolving mist."[7] That which is hurt and bound is healed and set free, and we find ourselves released from the limitations imposed upon us by that sin. This is what healing of memories is all about.

Dreams

The heart speaks to us in a symbolic language, and what is in it emerges in symbolic images or pictures. I at first misinterpreted the dreams that came to show me where my writer's block was located and made the mistake we are all apt to make if we attempt to understand our dreams on our own or without knowledge of how the dream speaks.[8] I was taking my unusual dreams too literally, was attempting to read them in the language of the rational, conscious mind. First looking at them, and before submitting them to the wise and prayerful scrutiny of my good friends, Herman and Lillie Riffel, I feared they were telling me I was some sort of showoff (exactly what Grandma would have thought!). Leaping rivers, acrobatic dancing, and high-wire artistry would be quite something for someone such as myself, a fairly dignified mother and grandmother at this point in time, and what's more, a little bit sedentary and given to prayer and scholarly pursuits.

Also, there *had been* a bridge very near my home; it was washed away by torrential waters when I was a small child. The memory of holding tight to my mother's hand and staring in amazement at the spot where the bridge had been and seeing only the angry brown waters roaring and tumbling is still vivid in me. But the bridge and creek bed, like and yet unlike the one I had known, imaged something far different from the literal effects of a spring storm. Lisa's dream of looking down and seeing a dark, black cancer through the pores of her skin imaged something very different from what that picture taken literally would imply. Matthew's dreams of homosexual involvement were not to be taken as saying, "You are homosexual." Moderns, not realizing that the dream speaks in a symbolic language, can very seriously misinterpret their dreams and thereby get into grave trouble. Yet this danger is quickly overcome when we hear the true interpretation, for our own hearts, in conjunction with the Holy Spirit, affirm it. This is why Herman Riffel can say,

> If an interpretation is right, the one who has had the dream will know it . . . for the dream is a confirmation of that which we already know. Therefore, never receive an interpretation of your own dream that your heart does not respond to.[9]

More about Dreams

The importance of dreams in helping to reveal and interpret these blocks has been pointed up by the examples given. The Scriptures repeatedly testify to the importance of the dream both as a revealer of the heart of man, and as a message-bearer with a word from God to that heart. Unfortunately, when we moderns pay attention to our dreams at all, we usually misunderstand the message they bear. There is a reason for this. We do not understand our two minds (our rational heads and our intuitive hearts) and their differing ways of *knowing*:

> Serious problems arise from our failure to understand and appreciate the ways of knowing peculiar to the so-called unconscious mind. This is the intuitive rather than the reasoning faculty, the seat of the creative imagination, the memory, and the gifts of the Holy Spirit. . . .
>
> This failure is . . . rooted in our inheritance of Greek thought, particularly from Aristotle. Aristotle's epistemology confirmed man's ways of receiving knowledge to the data received through his sense experience and his reason. By synthesizing experience, reason was thought capable of putting man in touch with the real. From these two ways of knowing (experience and reason), both belonging to the conscious mind, he developed his first principles of knowledge. He thus ruled out Plato's third way of knowing, which included the ways of divine inspiration, of the poet and the prophet, of the dream and the vision, and—most important of all—the way of love. These of course are the ways of the "unconscious" mind: the way of picture, metaphor, symbol, myth, and—with love—the way of Incarnation: that way which brings myth and fact together. Had this way of knowing been retained, we no doubt would not have the somewhat self-contradictory term "unconscious mind" in our vocabulary today, since this way is really not unconscious at all, but involves several different sorts of consciousness.
>
> As the Church, principally through St. Thomas Aquinas, came to accept the Aristotelian epistemology and incorporate it into its theology, the Judeo-Christian understanding of the deep heart (the unconscious mind and its ways of knowing) simply dropped from sight. There were no categories by which to recognize it. Christians and non-Christians alike came to value exclusively the conscious mind and its ways of knowing over those of the unconscious. This has not only greatly hampered the Western Christian's understanding of the creative imagination, but it has mightily suppressed our understanding of the work of the Holy Spirit in man. Indeed,

the development and integration of the whole man in his relationship to God, to other men, and to those things within himself have not been fully understood because of our failure to understand our two minds.[10]

The dream, as an intuitive way of knowing, is important therefore as a vehicle of *revelation*. What is in our hearts can thereby be revealed to our conscious minds. What is from the heart of God can via the dream be made known to our hearts and heads. The most important factor in dream interpretation, therefore, in its attempt to comprehend the symbolic language of the unconscious, is a complete dependence upon the Holy Spirit and the Word of God, and that in the company of others who are thus Spirit-led.

> The Holy Spirit, promised Christ, "shall lead you into all truth." Both man's reason and his imagination [his unconscious ways of knowing], apart from the indwelling Spirit, are lacking in Grace. Both need this infusion of the Holy Spirit and both need the wisdom and the balance provided only by the ingifted, indwelt Body Corporate. Here, in the Fellowship of the Holy Spirit, in light of the Holy Scriptures, are both reason and imagination to be verified.[11]

Any system of dream interpretation that does not presuppose the above will necessarily be based on a view of man and his unconscious (actually his differing levels of awareness) that differs to one extent or another from the Christian view. Unfortunately, the textbook study on dreams I could wholly recommend as both helpful and theologically sound has not yet appeared. In the meantime, it is important to be aware of the psychological and philosophical presuppositions underlying the existing writings on the subject. For example, knowing that Freud's presuppositions are naturalistic (i.e., that he has principally a biological view of man and his mind), we are not surprised to find a concentration on sex drives in his dream interpretation. Also, knowing that he viewed the unconscious more or less as a container of the unvalued and therefore repressed material of life, we don't expect him to see it as the seat of the creative imagination and the gifts of the Holy Spirit. The presuppositions of the material- ist are fairly easy to discern by the Christian lay-counselor, but most researchers and writers on dreams whom laymen read do not hold the biological view of man and mind that Freud did, but rather a humanist or even a supernaturalist view of some sort. The need to discern and distinguish these presuppositions about man and his mind from those of the Christian view is even greater. This is because they usually contain so much more that is helpful and true. The psychologist, Dr. C. G. Jung, for in- stance, probably knew more about man's "unconscious" ways of knowing than any other psychologist or philosopher living in modern times. He knew more about dreams, having as a scien- tist studied them for a lifetime. Unlike Freud, his friend and contemporary, he knew the unconscious to be the intuitive facul- ty for the creative imagination, the center from which knowl- edge other than that gained through experience and its synthesis by reason could flow. But helpful as Jung's insights can be, we must still keep in mind the fact that his presuppositions are not Christian—they are gnostic. Jung freely confesses himself to be gnostic, philosophically and psychologically. He used the bridge of medieval alchemy as a way into the gnosticism he chose to accept as a framework for his thought. The Christian who *uncrit- ically* introduces Jungian thought into Christian counseling and healing does a great disservice to the Body of Christ, for gnos- ticism is and always has been the worst enemy of Christianity. That is because, basically and finally, it is an interpretive system of subjective revelation, one that denies the Incarnation, and invariably ends in anthropocentricity and an erroneous view of God. Separated from the truth of the indwelling Christ by the Holy Spirit in man, it can end and often does in a psychic or "soulish" interpretation of unconscious revelation. By just such an interpretation of his own dreams, Jung deemed God to be both good and evil. In adopting uncritically Jung's theory of per- sonality structure, Christian counselors can quickly find themselves veering toward anthropocentric and humanistic psychologies of man. There will then be no place in their counseling for the Holy Spirit's power in healing, while at the same time there will be an open door for false revelation.

Oswald Chambers, speaking to the Christian says:

> Our personality is always too big for us to grasp. An island in the sea may be but the top of a great mountain. Personality is like an island. We know nothing about the great depths underneath; consequently we cannot estimate ourselves. We begin by thinking that we can, but we come to realize that there is only one Being who understands us, and that is our Creator. . . .
>
> Our Lord can never be defined in terms of individuality and independence, but only in terms of personality, "I and My Father are one." Personality merges, and you only reach your real identity when you are merged with another person. When love, or the Spirit of God strikes a man, he is transformed, he no longer insists upon his separate individuality. Our Lord never spoke in terms of individuality, of a man's . . . isolated position, but in terms of personality—"that they may be one, even as We are one."[12]

As Christians, our personality structure can only be considered in terms of Christ's indwelling Spirit. Ours is an incarnational view of man and reality, Christ in us, grace as it were, working in and through nature. The Holy Spirit, in concert with man's reason, yields the holy intellect; in concert with man's intuitive mind, the holy imagination. Our ways of knowing, conscious and unconscious, are thus wondrously gifted with the power of discernment. We can draw a line between revelation that is spiritual and true, and that which is merely psychic or "soulish." We can distinguish the word of truth from the words of the world, the flesh, and the devil.

Notes

Preface
[1]C. S. Lewis, "Weight of Glory," in *The Weight of Glory* (Grand Rapids, Mich.: Eerdmans, 1975), pp. 14, 15. (Published in England under the title *Transposition and Other Addresses.*)

1. Lisa's Story: Repressed Memory
[1]The healing of memories involves ministering with the healing gifts of the Spirit of God. This has not always been made sufficiently clear in writings on the subject.

[2]Fellatio is oral incorporation of the phallus.

[3]Agnes Sanford's phrase.

[4]Not all memories that need to be healed are repressed ones.

[5]Accidents or circumstances entirely beyond the control of the mother can cause such a traumatic break in her relationship to her infant. (For example, birth trauma, the absence of the mother, due to sickness or accident, in a moment of infantile stress before six months, and so on.)

[6]Leanne Payne, *Real Presence: The Holy Spirit in the Works of C. S. Lewis* (Westchester, Ill.: Cornerstone Books, 1979), pp. 57, 58.

[7]1 John 5:20, 21, NEB

[8]John 1:1, NEB.

[9]John 5:17, NIV.

[10]Luke 4:18, 19, NIV.

2. The Causes of Homosexuality: Contemporary Theories
[1]That two doctors in one locale would come up with the same judgment, particularly in view of Lisa's age, is I think a most unusual situation.

[2]"25 Propositions on a 75th Birthday," *New York Times*, April 24, 1978.

[3]E.g., Ruth Tiffany Barnhouse, whose *Homosexuality: A Symbolic Confusion* (New York: The Seabury Press, 1977) is recommended not only for its concise

182 / The Broken Image

and comprehensive insight and coverage of the homosexual problem itself, but for its responsible analyses of the other factors outside the scientific and medical that are contributing to the current demands to accept homosexuality as normal, therefore psychologically healthy and moral. As a responsible scholar and researcher, she exposes inadequate arguments along with their faulty presuppositions and statistical data, and thereby takes the spurious scientific mask off much of the current jargon. In addition, she puts the whole problem in its historical perspective, and as both practicing psychiatrist and theologian, she recognizes when the various issues are outside their proper scientific and/or moral domain. Her recommendations for further reading as well as her footnotes comprise as fine a bibliography on both sides of the issues at hand as one could want.

[4]*Ibid.*, pp. 116, 117.

[5]Actually this is a message that continues to be pointed up to us. We found we were largely powerless to help a generation of young people caught in drugs and the occult.

[6]Communications Department, Episcopal Diocese of Atlanta, 2744 Peachtree Road N.W., Atlanta, Georgia 30305.

3. Matthew's Story: Identity Crisis

[1]C. S. Lewis, *Surprised by Joy: The Shape of My Early Life* (New York: Harcourt, Brace and World, 1955), p. 71.

[2]See Payne, *Real Presence*, Chapter 7.

[3]The true or the higher self is the essential self in union with God. It partakes richly of Him. In relation to God, this self (whether it be of the man-soul or the woman-soul) has always been understood to be feminine. "What is above and beyond all things is so masculine that we are all feminine in relation to it." (C. S. Lewis, *That Hideous Strength: A Modern Fairy-Tale for Grown-ups* [New York: Collier, 1962], p. 316)

[4]Matthew, in earlier dreams that predated the homosexual compulsions, had dreamt of other young men, all of whom he greatly admired and for the same reasons. In these dreams he would go to them and kiss them lightly on the mouth. After his healing and several years later, he told me that the phallic fantasy came later, and that it was "a vulgarization of the kissing fantasy that came about as I heard about homosexuality."

[5](New York: Paulist Press, 1974), p. 51.

[6]*The Virtues* (Chicago: Regnery Company, 1967), p. 6.

[7]Ephesians 4:23, NEB.

[8]Galatians 5:22, NEB.

[9]Psalm 86:11.

[10]Oswald Chambers, writing in *My Utmost for His Highest* (New York: Dodd, Mead and Co., n.d.), says, "One of the reasons of stultification in prayer is that there is no imagination, no power of putting ourselves deliberately before God." (February 10)

[11]Agnes Sanford taped message on sexual problems.

[12](Downers Grove, Ill.: InterVarsity Press, 1978), p. 8.

[13]Guido Groeger, as quoted by Walter Trobisch, *Love Yourself*, p. 9.

[14]Walter Trobisch, *Love Yourself*, p. 15.

[15]*Ibid.*, pp. 14, 15.

[16]How much better was our old term for this: the virtue of self-acceptance! It was much easier to image, and better sounding to the ear. It held moral value.

[17]*Clinical Theology* (London: Darton, Longman and Todd, 1966), pp. 724-728.

[18]This is why Church and parents have throughout history come down so hard (often with little wisdom or understanding) on sex-play in children. Curiosity in sexual matters can so quickly turn into something other than mere intellectual interest. For instance, it is not unusual to pray with someone who is overtly homosexual and find the root memory (i.e., the incident in which the homosexuality began) to be that of youthful curiosity and masturbation and/or group masturbation and sex-play.

[19]Heaven and all it contains, according to Lewis, is of such reality that the unredeemed (those who have chosen self and Hell) can never be at home in it. In *The Great Divorce* (New York: Macmillan, 1971), he pictures those who refuse redemption as insubstantial and even ghostlike.

[20]*Ibid.*, p. 91.

[21]*Ibid.*, p. 101.

[22]See Payne, *Real Presence*, pp. 139-141.

4. The Search for Sexual Identity

[1]Payne, *Real Presence*, pp. 68-70, 72, 116, 117, 135-145, 149-157.

[2]*Ibid.*, pp. 166-168.

[3]Oil that is, in the Anglican and Roman communions, blessed by the bishop and set apart specifically for the laying on of hands and prayer for the healing of the sick in mind or body.

[4]"Humble yourselves—feeling very insignificant—in the presence of the Lord, and He will exalt you. He will lift you up and make your lives significant" (James 4:10, *Amplified*).

[5]Isaiah 26:3.

[6]There are those who deliberately try to cast such an image of themselves, but their need is different to Jay's in that they are attempting to crystallize their failure to differentiate their sexual identity from that of the mother. These are the ones who so often do not seek help until they've done great damage to themselves psychologically and physically. E.g., these men may seek and find sexual conversions through surgery and hormonal drugs, irremedial measures that are all too often made available to them before they find the healing they need.

[7]A rejection need not always be brought to conscious awareness to be healed through prayer. The person will simply know a peace and a freedom from the problem he has not known before.

[8]In the severest cases, as we shall see in the grouping "Homosexual and Lesbian Behavior Related to Failure of the Infant to Achieve an Adequate Sense of Being," it can render the infant unable to receive its mother's love—a position of being schizoid in relation to her.

[9]It is also easy to see how such an infant could desire death to the pain involved in such a struggle to live. There is, at times, within such sufferers a

death wish to be dealt with. In the case of breech birth trauma, there are healings that indicate the infant does not *want* to be born and resists leaving the womb. In these cases, there seems to be an intuitive *knowing* of what lies ahead in the full acceptance of one's vocation in life. This is so according to Barbara Shlemon and others who, like herself, were born breech and have experienced the type of healing described above in regard to the circumstances of their birth.

[10]Acts 3:1-10.

[11]Letter (March 6, 1956) to a Mr. Masson, Wade Collection, Wheaton College, Wheaton, Illinois.

[12]Payne, *Real Presence*, p. 141.

[13]Barnhouse, *Homosexuality: A Symbolic Confusion*, p. 26.

[14]*Ibid.*, p. 27.

[15]Payne, *Real Presence*, pp. 170, 171.

[16]Nobel lecture, 1973.

[17]C. S. Lewis, *Mere Christianity* (New York: Macmillan, 1964), pp. 94, 95.

[18]Chambers, *My Utmost for His Highest*, p. 363.

[19]1 Samuel 15:23, KJV.

[20]Romans 12:19, KJV.

[21]One of the women wrote to me later that within this devouring love was the "craving to be craved, to be wanted, idolized, adored, glorified, possessed, noticed, admired, along with the craving to control, to possess."

[22]Lewis, *The Great Divorce*, p. 89. See especially Chapters 10, 11 (Lewis's character sketches of Hilda and Pam).

[23]This principle is brought into disrepute only when we come to care merely for the outer image. Christ addressed this problem when He said: "Woe unto you, scribes and Pharisees, hypocrites! For ye are like unto whited sepulchres, which indeed appear beautiful outward, but are within full of dead men's bones, and of all uncleanness. Even so ye also outwardly appear righteous unto men, but within ye are full of hypocrisy and iniquity" (Matthew 23:27, 28, KJV).

[24]Emma Curtis Hopkins, *High Mysticism* (Del Rey, Calif.: De Vorss, 1974).

[25]This I've seen to be the case in such thinking persons as college professors. It strikes me as paradoxical to see the sexualized identity in a woman whose intellect has been highly developed, but such is the case until psychological healing takes place.

[26]Quoted from the J. R. R. Tolkien essay "On Fairy Stories."

[27]*Ibid.*

[28]*Reaching Out* (New York: Doubleday, 1966), p. 22.

[29]*Ibid.*

[30]In the psychological sense of hysterical clinging to another person.

[31]See especially Chapter 4, "The Understanding and Treatment of Hysterical Personalities," and Chapter 10, "Homosexuality: The Development of an Androcentric Personality."

[32]*Ibid.*, p. 9.

[33]*Ibid.*, p. 10.

[34]*Ibid.*, p. 940.

[35]Such a sufferer does not always run, as one reminds me when she writes: "I reached out time and time again for help, but no one seemed able to help. I

was twenty-nine years of age before I fell into the defense pattern of relating to other women and [after that] I was eight years under psychiatric help and in complete darkness with depression."

[36]Hebrews 10:19, NIV.

[37]Quoted by Ruth Pitter, see Letters to Ruth Pitter, p. 2, Wade Collection, Wheaton College, Wheaton, Illinois.

[38]A copy of this letter may be seen in the Wade Collection, Wheaton College, Wheaton, Illinois. The original is in the Bodlein Library, Oxford. It also appears in Sheldon Vanauken, *A Severe Mercy* (New York: Harper & Row, 1977), pp. 146, 147.

[39]Lake, *Clinical Theology*, p. 932.

[40]*Ibid.*, p. 933.

[41]*Ibid.*, p. 401.

[42]*Ibid.*, p. 429.

[43]*Ibid.*, p. 984.

5. The Identity Crisis According to the Scriptures

[1]Colossians 2:9, 10, NEB.

[2]"Membership," *The Weight of Glory*, p. 40.

[3]Matthew 16:13-19.

[4]Mark 8:34, 36, NEB.

[5]See Payne, *Real Presence*, Chapter 7, "The Great Dance."

[6]*The Four Loves* (New York: Harcourt, Brace and Co., 1960), Chapter 1.

[7]Study the character of Mark Studdock in C. S. Lewis, *That Hideous Strength*.

[8]Romans 1:19-25, NEB.

[9]Romans 2:14-16, NEB.

[10]Mother Theresa of Calcutta is perhaps one of the greatest examples of this truth in our day. She functions in God's image, doing what the world can only deem the impossible, and this miracle of love comes directly out of her adoration and commitment to her Lord.

[11]Hebrews 10:19, NIV.

[12]Romans 1:2, NEB.

6. Listening for the Healing Word

[1]A vision that seems to involve even the sensory powers, one in which the physical eyes seem to have, for an instant, a heightened perception.

[2]The imperative prayer of the earliest Christians.

[3]Lewis, *The Four Loves*, p. 174.

[4]"Silence, the Portable Cell," *Sojourners*, July 1980.

[5]2 Timothy 3:15, NEB.

[6]Matthew 4:4, NIV.

[7]Ephesians 6:14, 15, NEB.

[8]Acts 17:11, 12, NEB.

[9]Romans 5:5, NEB.

[10]Ephesians 3:18, 19, NEB.

[11]Psalm 95:7, NEB.

[12]Isaiah 11:3, 4, NIV.

[13]See John 8:28, 29.

[14]Ephesians 6:17, NEB.

[15]C. S. Lewis, *Letters to Malcolm: Chiefly on Prayer* (New York: Harcourt, Brace and World, 1963), n.p.

[16]Psalm 90:8, NEB.

[17]Lake, *Clinical Theology*, p. 40.

[18]*Ibid.*

[19]C. S. Lewis, *Christian Reflections* (Grand Rapids, Mich.: Eerdmans, 1971), p. 169.

[20]Luke 11:34, KJV.

[21]This first appeared in *Sharing* magazine, the Order of St. Luke's journal on healing, August 1950.

[22]Lewis, *Mere Christianity*, pp. 168, 169.

[23]*The Gulag Archipelago* II, Part IV, Chapter I, "Ascent" (New York: Harper and Row, 1975), n.p.

[24]Romans 8:12, JB.

[25]Romans 8:12, 13, NEB.

[26]C. S. Lewis, *Reflections of the Soul* (New York: Harcourt, Brace and World, 1958), pp. 31, 32.

[27]*The Gulag Archipelago*, Part IV, Chapter I, n.p.

[28]C. S. Lewis, *The Pilgrim's Regress: An Allegorical Apology for Christianity, Reason and Romanticism* (Grand Rapids, Mich.: Eerdmans, 1973).

[29]Payne, *Real Presence*, pp. 71, 72.

[30]*Reaching Out*, p. 22.

[31]*Ibid.*

[32]*Ibid.*

[33]Isaiah 64:7.

[34]For a study of the true imagination, see Payne, *Real Presence*, Chapters 10 ("The Whole Imagination I: Surprised by Joy") and 11 ("The Whole Imagination II: The Two Minds").

[35]*Ibid.*, pp. 131, 132, quoting *The Oxford English Dictionary*, compact edition, s.v. "imagination."

[36]*Ibid.*, pp. 136, 137.

[37]See C. S. Lewis, *The Problem of Pain* (New York: Macmillan, 1966), Chapter 1.

[38]Payne, *Real Presence*, p. 137.

[39]C. S. Lewis, "Dogma and the Universe," *God in the Dock: Essays on Theology and Ethics* (Grand Rapids, Mich.: Eerdmans, 1970).

[40]*My Utmost for His Highest*, February 11.

[41]*Ibid.*, February 10.

[42]1 Corinthians 12:4-11.

[43]Galatians 5:22, 23.

[44]C. S. Lewis's great mythic novel *Perelandra* (New York: Collier, 1962) images the Great Dance in Chapter 17.

[45]Lewis, *The Problem of Pain*, p. 139.

[46]"It says in the Bible that the whole universe was made for Christ and that

everything is to be gathered into Him." Lewis doesn't know how this applies to things other than men, but he likes to imagine "that when intelligent creatures entered into Christ they would, in that way, bring all the other things in along with them [all creation in man]. But I do not know: it is only a guess." (*Mere Christianity*, p. 170)

Appendix: Listening to Our Dreams

[1]Psalm 16:7.

[2]A writer's block is never simply a writer's block. Once freed, one finds himself also freer in other areas.

[3]Unbelief and failure to trust God, of course, were the sins to be confessed, those behind the emotion of fear.

[4]I cannot certainly say this was so, but in retrospect this seems highly probable.

[5]See Payne, *Real Presence*, Chapters 5, 6, 7.

[6]Psalm 19:12, *Amplified*.

[7]Isaiah 44:22, NEB.

[8]For a study of dreams in the context of how God speaks to us, I should like to recommend Herman H. Riffel, *Voice of God: The Significance of Dreams, Visions, Revelations* (Wheaton, Ill.: Tyndale House, 1978). Also, Karen Burton Mains, *The Key to a Loving Heart* (Elgin, Ill.: David C. Cook, 1979), Chapter 4, on the role of the dream as a message-bearer.

[9]Riffel, *Voice of God*, p. 85.

[10]Payne, *Real Presence*, Chapter 11, "The Whole Imagination II: The Two Minds."

[11]*Ibid.*

[12]*Chambers, My Utmost for His Highest*, December 12, p. 347.

Crisis In Masculinity

by Leanne Payne

Distorted personalities; ineffectual husbands, fathers too busy or remote to spend time with their families; men unfulfilled at work or at home. Many men today are utterly confused about their identity, fearful of authority and fearful of God. The role models have gone, and with them the old certainties.

The consequences can be appalling. Unaffirmed men cannot affirm their sons'—or their daughters'—sexuality. They frequently remain immature and become increasingly passive, unable to lift themselves or their families out of the quagmires of life.

Leanne Payne clearly identifies the problem and its roots, and, with a wealth of illustration from her own ministry as a counsellor, shows how men can rediscover their identity and be restored to wholeness. This book concerns the healing of men, but it also offers hope for women, since the feminine and the masculine complement one another.

Kingsway Publications

The Healing Presence

by Leanne Payne

'Biblical, practical, penetrating and personal...a unique contribution to the literature on healing and counselling.'
—*Michael Cole*

Leanne Payne, in the course of her long ministry, has found that the single largest factor keeping people from experiencing the riches that God has in store for them is the failure to forgive and to receive forgiveness. This barrier poisons relationships and destroys our joy in living. Yet, as we learn to practise the Presence of Jesus, we begin to live fully and see His power change our lives.

Mrs Payne's own experience of the Healing Presence of Christ is crucial to her understanding of forgiveness. 'There, in His presence, as one would spread an extremely valuable but shattered vase before a master craftsman, I could dare to spread out the broken pieces of my mind and heart. There, in fullest confidence in His healing love, my eyes fixed on Him in obedience, I watched as He not only mended my broken heart but united it with His.'

'I gulped drafts of living water as I read.'
—*John White*

'A gold mine of wisdom. It should become priority reading for all Christian counsellors.'
—*David and Mary Pytches*

MRS LEANNE PAYNE is founder and president of Pastoral Care Ministries, and a regular speaker in the UK. She is author of *The Broken Image*, *Crisis in Masculinity* and *Real Presence*.

Kingsway Publications

Restoring The Chrisian Soul

by Leanne Payne

Time and again Leanne Payne has discovered that
Christians meet three barriers as they move towards the
goal of personal wholeness and maturity, finding
themselves unable to—
> —accept themselves
> —forgive others
> —receive forgiveness.

Building on the theological and psychological foundations
laid in *The Healing Presence*, Leanne Payne charts the way
to overcoming those barriers through the power of healing
prayer.

'In this book and *The Healing Presence*, Leanne Payne gives us the
most comprehensive and helpful work on soul healing I know.
Christians who require healing or who minister healing to others
need these books.'

—KEN BLUE
Author of *Authority to Heal*

'A masterful book that helps Christian leaders establish the cross
firmly in all aspects of their lives and ministries.'

—ANDREW COMISKEY
Director of Desert Stream Ministries

Mrs Leanne Payne is founder and president of Pastoral Care
Ministries, and author of *The Broken Image, Crisis in Masculinity*
and *The Healing Presence*.

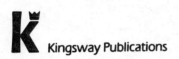

Kingsway Publications